The Tao of Twitter

Changing Your Life and Business
140 Characters at a Time

Mark W. Schaefer

New York   Chicago   San Francisco   Lisbon   London
Madrid   Mexico City   Milan   New Delhi   San Juan   Seoul
Singapore   Sydney   Toronto

1 2 3 4 5 6 7 8 9 0   DOC/DOC   1 8 7 6 5 4 3 2

ISBN: 978-0-07-180219-2
MHID: 0-07-180219-3

e-ISBN: 978-0-07-180220-8
e-MHID: 0-07-180220-7

An earlier version of this book (ISBN 978-06154732-3) was published in 2011 by Create Space.

McGraw-Hill books are available at special quantity discounts to use as premiums and sales promotions, or for use in corporate training programs. To contact a representative please e-mail us at bulksales@mcgraw-hill.com.

Contents

Introduction

When I bought my first desktop computer, it came with two sets of instructions.

The first set was a simple color-coded poster to help you know how to plug in the mouse, the keyboard, and the monitor, so you could get up and running in a matter of minutes.

The second was a hefty booklet that described the software basics, shortcuts, and practical tools to help you really make the device useful.

Studies show that about 60 percent of the people who try Twitter quit after the first week, and I'm convinced it's because they never get past the first set of simple instructions: set up a profile, follow a few celebrities, tweet about "what you're doing now," and see what happens.

Problem is . . . the second set of instructions doesn't exist.

Until now. And that's why we're here.

Twitter has changed my life and the lives of hundreds of my clients, readers, and students. Where so many others have quit or failed, we are enjoying the benefits of the most powerful business networking system that has ever existed.

It isn't just a cute kiddie-toy or chat function for keeping in touch with friends. With its real-time human-driven results, Twitter has become the networking, information, and search engine of choice for many business professionals. Why? Twitter can help you:

- Attract new audiences and potential customers, partners, and suppliers
- Follow news on your industry, market, competition, and customers
- Solve problems quickly
- Stay on top of the latest research, opinion, insights, and competitive intelligence
- Learn new skills
- Strengthen new and existing business relationships
- Open up low-cost marketing opportunities

Sadly, most people miss this completely, because they don't know what I know and what my students have discovered.

They haven't found the path, the Tao of Twitter.

Since the first edition was published, in early 2011, thousands of people from around the world have benefited from this book. Nearly every day I receive a message (most frequently in the form of a tweet!) thanking me for "opening my world times ten," as one fan put it. I'm delighted you've joined our movement!

If you're completely new to Twitter, I recommend that you read this book from start to finish. If you're a pro, feel free to jump around and collect some new ideas along the way.

Let's get started!

CHAPTER ONE

Discovering the Tao of Twitter

The first tweet I ever received was: "It's 4 a.m."

Obviously, Twitter and I did not get off to a good start! Like most people, I thought it was just about the stupidest thing I had ever tried and that first tweet seemed to confirm it.

But I stuck with it, because, as a consultant and marketing educator, I was determined to learn what the buzz was about. I thought the whole thing was a little silly and maybe even spooky when unknown "followers" just started showing up.

And then I had my "a-ha" moment.

I was bored and was playing around on the computer one night when I logged on to Twitter and clicked on a trending topic for #NewFluName. I knew enough by this time to know that these topics represented the most popular real-time conversations in the world. Mildly curious, I clicked to see what was happening. It was a moment I'll never forget.

Remember when the pork industry was having a fit about the swine flu a few years ago? They thought the name was hurting sales of "the other white meat" and asked the public to call it something else. So thousands of people from around the world tweeted their contributions— HILARIOUS new names, like,

- The Aporkalypse
- Porky's Revenge
- This little piggy went to the bathroom
- Hog Flashes
- Porkenstein
- The Other White Flu
- Mad Sow Disease
- Hamageddon
- and my favorite, "Hamthrax"

Yes, it broke the monotony of my evening . . . in fact, I laughed until I cried! But something more important happened. I was witnessing a real-time, global brainstorming session! It dawned on me that at no other time in the history of mankind could that conversation have taken place. It was an awesome moment, an inspiring moment. I began to think about all of the implications for business, for networking, for solving problems, for learning . . . and for me.

People sharing, connecting, teaching, and entertaining each other in the moment—from every corner of the world. I had caught a glimpse of something profound and wonderful.

Over the next several weeks I witnessed Twitter serve as a powerful news source during the revolutionary activity in Iran (which put it on the cover of *Time* magazine). I made my first meaningful business connections. A torrent of links, humor, and insights came rushing at me every day, as I learned to surround myself with thought-leaders, teachers, and innovators. I began to realize that Twitter was probably the most dynamic, interesting, and compelling educational tool I had ever seen.

And the journey was just beginning . . .

- My region of the United States is prone to dangerous storm cells and tornadoes. As the fierce winds arrived one day, we lost power and all communication . . . except for Twitter, where I could read reports from local friends on the status of flooding and damage in the area. A tweet from a friend suggested an NOAA emergency weather center iPhone app that broadcast radio news during the storm, which I downloaded immediately.

- Through Twitter I have connected to hundreds of inspiring people from around the world, but none perhaps as loyal and dedicated as a young man named Muhammad Saad Khan, who is using Twitter and the social web to learn about social media from his home in Karachi, Pakistan. When I learned that he could not obtain a copy of my book, I sent him one. He is now using my book to teach others in his country how to use social media effectively.

- A Twitter friend knew I was teaching college courses in social media and recommended me to one of his clients, resulting in a consulting engagement with the U.K. government.

- After struggling with a problem with my blog RSS feed for a week, I asked for help over Twitter, and within minutes I found a resource that had the problem solved in one hour.

- One of my students, a music teacher, was able to promote her videos and connect to new friends associated with a well-known folk music festival in Texas. Through these relationships, she was invited to perform at the annual event. "This is my dream come true," she told me. "And it could not have happened any other way. Twitter has changed my life."

- I founded an annual social media conference called Social Slam, which attracts hundreds of people from throughout the U.S. and beyond. We sell this conference out each year and have never spent one dime on advertising. Every participant learned of the event through the powerful word-of-mouth attraction of Twitter.

I could go on, but by now I hope you're starting to see the diversity, usefulness, profitability, power, and fun of Twitter.

Make no mistake, there is a Tao to Twitter. There is a majestic random synergy that holds the potential to affect your life daily—if you know what you're doing. And most people don't know what they're doing. They don't grasp the Tao.

If you dissect any successful Twitter case study, any business benefit, any personal accomplishment that started with a tweet, there is a common theme—a success formula of sorts. The more I have become immersed in the social web, the more I am convinced that this Tao, or formula, is the path to success on Twitter.

By nature, I'm a conservative person. I'm not prone to bold claims. But after seeing hundreds, maybe thousands, of people follow the advice in this book, *I know* it works.

Our generation's source of all wisdom—that would be Wikipedia, of course—defines Tao as a word that "literally translates as 'way,' 'path,' or 'route' generally used to signify the primordial essence or fundamental aspect of the universe."

I like that idea. So let's explore this path . . . this primordial essence. But to best explain it, I need help from a young graduate student and my favorite football team.

CHAPTER TWO

The Tao of Twitter in Action

One October evening I was watching my favorite American football team—the Pittsburgh Steelers—and doing a little work-related multi-tasking. I flipped on Twitter and announced through a Twitter message (known as a tweet): "Watching a football game tonight—Go Steelers!"

A few moments later I received a reply from Michelle Chmielewski (or, @MiChmksi as she is known on Twitter), who was at that time a graduate student at the University of Pittsburgh. "Watching the game too! Hope we will win!" she tweeted back at me.

Now, I only had a vague idea of who this person was. Although we had "followed" each other on Twitter, I could not recall ever having any dialogue with her before and certainly had no indication that this random tweet was about to change the course of our lives.

But Michelle knew who I was. Like any smart networker, she had taken care to surround herself with people she could learn from. Because I was a marketing professional, blogger, and college educator, she had included me in her Twitter tribe, and now took this opportunity to reach out and connect on a very human subject—sports. She wasn't selling anything. She wasn't asking for anything. She was simply being herself.

About a week later I was surprised and delighted to receive an e-mail from Michelle: "It was nice getting to 'meet' you the other night on Twitter," she wrote. "I really admire what you're doing on your blog, Mark. I am just starting out as a blogger myself. My blog is called 'The Observing Participant.' Is there any way you could take a look at what I am doing and give me some feedback?"

Of course I was happy to look at her work, and what I found astonished me. Michelle was creating innovative video blogs that were unlike anything I had seen. Her content was funny, quirky, and edgy, telling a story in a very entertaining and compelling fashion. I went through post after post, and I was convinced I had discovered an amazing talent.

I began to mention her posts in my tweets, because I believed in what she was doing and wanted to help her get some exposure. After a few weeks, I had the brilliant idea of asking Michelle to actually make one of her charming videos for my new company. Wouldn't that be a unique way to tell *my* story and explain what I do?

Michelle said she was interested in the project, but felt funny about taking money from her new "mentor." She mentioned that she needed a new high-definition video camera to continue her work, so I offered to purchase one for her as a way to help her further her career. She picked out the camera of her choice and my video was on its way. I was so pleased about the success that I wrote a little blog post about it to celebrate. Although Michelle looks back on this video as being a little crude compared to what she's producing today, it's still on my site as a testament to the beginning of our wonderful friendship.

The Benefits Multiply

Little did I know that the business benefits of this Twitter connection were just starting!

At a networking meeting in Pittsburgh, Michelle met the owner of a start-up company who desperately needed some marketing help. "I know just the guy," she told him and set up a call for me to talk with the entrepreneur.

Now I was a little too busy to take on this business, but I knew just the person who could—my friend Trey

Pennington,* somebody I had also met through a random tweet. Just as Michelle had included me in her "tribe," I had mindfully sought out this connection with Trey, whom I regarded as a mentor and teacher.

After exchanging tweets with Trey for some time, I had moved our online relationship into an offline friendship when I met him for lunch in his home state of South Carolina. During our visit, he told me that the recession in his area had taken a toll on his business and he was looking for work. Trey was grateful for the opportunity and followed up with the new business lead in Pittsburgh. He had a new customer!

I explained to Trey how I had discovered Michelle and he was also deeply impressed by her singular talent. "Can you introduce me?" he asked. "I'd like to have her on my show."

Trey produced a thought-provoking podcast called *The Marketing Professor* and soon was featuring Michelle and her innovative ideas for using video as a storytelling medium on blogs.

With the popular blog post, the radio show, and the rush of new traffic to her blog, Michelle's star was rising fast!

---

* Tragically, Trey died a few months after the first edition of this book came out, in 2011. He loved *The Tao of Twitter* and this story of our collaboration so much that I decided to keep this case study in all future editions of the book, as an everlasting tribute to his kindness, leadership, and friendship.

As her college graduation neared, Michelle was offered a job with a social-media software company in Paris. She had never had to consider a life-changing offer like this before, and she turned to me as a mentor to ask for my advice before responding.

She soon became a successful community manager and her growing company needed a foothold in the United States. They needed to hire a new business development manager. "I know just the guy," she said, and recommended that they call me about the opportunity.

My consulting business was strong, and I couldn't take on this additional work, but I recommended that they also talk to Trey, who was already on their radar screen because of Michelle. They flew Trey to London for a meeting and offered him the position.

Over the months Michelle, Trey, and I had opportunities to help and support each other in numerous ways. It could be something as important as a career choice or as simple as pinging Michelle on Skype to get help with a video editing problem.

Going Global

When my wife and I were planning a trip to France, we made a special effort to stay a night in Paris to meet Michelle. While it was a great thrill to finally see her in person, the visit was even more interesting because it coincided with a party she helped plan for a number of bloggers from around the world. Under a bridge. Next to Notre Dame. With champagne.

It was a magical night, as I compared notes and exchanged cards with fascinating social media entrepreneurs from Europe, Canada, Asia, and South America. One of my new acquaintances was seeking a permanent job in the U.S. and needed a letter of recommendation, which I was happy to provide.

I also became friends with Gregory Pouy, one of France's most outstanding marketing bloggers. Soon, Gregory was translating his amazing eBooks into English, so that I could offer them exclusively on my blog. This provided exceptional new content for my readers and a new global audience for Greg.

Can you begin to sense the energy flowing though this experience?

Can you see the relationships blooming, the business benefits building like an avalanche rolling down a steep mountain? And remember, it started with one stray tweet, "Go Steelers!"

It seems like a lot of luck was involved for all of this to happen, right?

Wrong.

This was not luck. This exchange was enabled by The Tao of Twitter, the secret sauce that experienced social web networkers and marketers sense but may not be able to name or explain. There is an underlying wisdom that created this success story, and thousands of others like it.

Let's use this fun little story to explain the formula, the Tao of Twitter.

CHAPTER THREE

The Tao
Explained

I have studied, observed, and written about hundreds of
different success stories involving Twitter and the social web,
and they all have one common formula running through
them. This is truly the path, the way, the Tao of Twitter.

Business benefits are created through three elements:

Targeted Connections +

Meaningful Content +

Authentic Helpfulness

Let's see how this worked in the real world.

Targeted Connections

No amount of work, time, or dedication to marketing
and social media networking will work if you haven't

surrounded yourself with people who might be interested in you and what you have to say.

So, while it might seem like the Mark-Michelle-Trey-Gregory story was random, the conditions were ripe for this connection, because all four of us had systematically surrounded ourselves with people likely to want to know us, learn from us, and help us.

In the next chapter, we'll go through many ideas on how to create these conditions for yourself. Networking doesn't occur by chance in the traditional business world, and it doesn't occur by chance alone on the social web either.

In the "Go Steelers" story, Michelle, Trey, Gregory, and I had *purposefully selected each other* at some point in the past, even though we had no idea what, if anything, might become of it in the future. That's the majestic random synergy of Twitter that I mentioned earlier.

Think of Twitter followers as atoms flying around inside of a chemist's test tube, bumping into each other randomly. Obviously, the more atoms you have in the tube, the better your chances that a reaction will occur!

But every chemical reaction needs a catalyst, and on Twitter that catalyst is . . .

Meaningful Content

Content is the currency of the social web, and sharing that content is the catalyst to new relationships and business benefits.

Let's look at the role of meaningful content in this story. What was the content that created these powerful connections?

Tweets

Our first connection came through my simple tweet about a football game. There's an important truth here. My tweet was not a Ph.D. thesis, a white paper, or even a blog post. But it was meaningful to the person receiving it.

This is a lesson that is lost on many people trying to network on the social web. They have highly-engineered content aimed at certain buyer personas. And while there is value to this—both in theory and practice—networking and marketing on the social web isn't about search engine optimization or keywords or B2B or B2C, it's all about *P2P—person to person connections.*

Social media is SOCIAL.

There is a high value for authenticity and being human on Twitter, a lesson I learned early on. Like a classic marketer, I wanted to "reach" my "targeted audience" with well-defined "messaging." But at some point, I relaxed and was just me. At that crossroad, a wonderful breakthrough occurred. Instead of trying to find my audience and customers, they found me. *Twitter is about content for humans, not search engines.*

Blogs

Blogs and Twitter fit like a hand in a glove. Twitter is like the trailer to the blog's movie.

No matter how you describe it, the tweets about my blog attracted Michelle's attention, and it was this content—highly meaningful to her as a fellow marketer— that created an incentive for her to take the next step in the relationship, to connect and ask for help.

Likewise, her content (video blogs) definitely attracted my attention, too. Blogs can play an important role in this respect. Profiles, status updates, and résumés may *indicate* that you know your stuff but blogs *demonstrate* that you know it!

I also used my ability to create content on my blog to showcase Michelle and her formidable video talents.

Greg's blog content earned my respect and was featured on my blog, creating awareness for him to an entirely new global audience.

Links

For the sake of brevity, I didn't get into the daily details of our Twitter relationship, but Michelle, Trey, Gregory, and I stayed in each other's orbits through interesting and helpful links we tweet each day. These tweets could link to articles, videos, photographs—just about any kind of content that would be interesting and useful.

Other kinds of content that served as catalysts for business benefits were Trey's podcasts, Michelle's videos, and Gregory's eBooks.

And finally, none of this would have happened without . . .

Authentic Helpfulness

This third and final factor is the one that is most misused, misunderstood, and simply ignored by most folks using Twitter today. There is an extremely important and subtle difference between traditional sales/marketing and the new media. I think it can be best illustrated through this question: Do you believe that at any time in this evolving relationship my aim was to sell my professional services to Michelle? Were any of us trying to sell anything to anybody?

I hope you replied "no," and if you did, you're on your way to understanding this very crucial aspect of the new-media marketing mindset.

At least for the foreseeable future, there will be a place for cold calling and the traditional sales function. When you schedule a call with a new client in many industries, he or she expects you to go through a tailored and well-rehearsed sales pitch.

But that simply doesn't work on the social web. People are sick of being sold to, marketed to, and tricked into clicking on links to unwanted products.

In an always-on, real-time, global world of business communications, the priority is on *human interaction* that leads to connections. Connections lead to awareness. Awareness leads to trust. Trust is the ultimate catalyst to business benefits, as it always has been.

I'm going to devote a chapter to each of these three integrated elements of the Tao of Twitter. None of them can succeed independently of the others.

Before we dive into these important concepts and learn some practical applications, let's take a closer look at what we're really after here.

Why are we doing this? What are the business benefits of Twitter?

CHAPTER FOUR

The Business Benefits of Twitter

In the case study I used to illustrate the Tao of Twitter, not one direct sale was made, and yet I believe you'll agree that the personal and business benefits were powerful and undeniable. They included:

- Michelle receiving feedback on her blog and videos
- A new HD video camera for Michelle
- A mentoring relationship for Michelle
- A new company video for my website
- Blog post content for Mark
- New blog subscribers for Michelle
- Podcast content for Trey
- Publicity for Michelle
- A new customer for Trey
- Job advice for Michelle

- A marketing position for Trey
- Support on video technical problems for Mark
- An invitation to a Paris party for Mark
- New international blogging connections for Mark
- Global brand awareness for Gregory
- Exclusive new content for Mark from Gregory
- A work visa recommendation for Michelle's friend
- A chapter for this book
- And most important for all of us, supportive friendships that will last throughout the years

And all of this occurred within 18 months! Now, look through this list. How many of these benefits are easily quantifiable? How many could be displayed on a graph or pie chart? We need to begin expanding our minds about the possible benefits of business on the social web.

I'm spending time discussing the business benefits of Twitter because this is where most companies miss a big opportunity. They don't want to devote resources to an activity without a measurable return on investment.

And for many well-managed companies, this mindset has worked exceptionally well in the past. But if you look at the list above and other potential benefits of Twitter such as:

- Competitive intelligence
- Market insight

- A new supplier or partner
- Publicity
- Brand awareness
- An idea
- New products and services
- And yes, even a potential customer

. . . most of these benefits are intangible and difficult to display in an Excel spreadsheet! So why keep trying to do it? Many of the benefits of the social web are *qualitative*, not *quantitative*. Here's another example.

I once recognized somebody at a networking meeting from his Twitter picture. Because I had been following his tweets, I knew that he had just started a new online business, had two little boys, had recently vacationed in California, and was a baseball fanatic. I had never met him before in my life, but when I introduced myself, he gave me a bear-hug and greeted me like a long lost friend! Through my stream of information on Twitter, he felt he knew me, too. We had formed a connection that led to friendship and trust.

The meeting was about to start, and we didn't have time to chat, but we exchanged phone numbers and committed to meet for coffee, to talk about ways we could work together. He eventually became one of my best customers.

Now, how many cold calls would you have to make to find a new business connection who greets you with a hug on the first meeting? I had effectively used Twitter to *pre-populate the business relationship!* And yes, it did eventually result in sales, but more important, it resulted in a new business connection that can create opportunities for years to come.

You Must Measure

Please don't misunderstand. I'm not saying you don't need to measure social media marketing efforts if you are using this tool for a business. You absolutely do. I'm an old-school data junkie, and I believe everything we do in marketing needs to be tied to the creation of value for the business in some way.

And it *may* be possible for you to calculate a Return on Investment (ROI)—(which is strictly a financial measure by the way!). But if you *only* look at ROI, you're going to be missing the bigger picture, and you'll be left in the dust by smarter competitors.

For this reason, I think small businesses have an advantage over big companies in this space. As a small-business owner, I don't find it necessary to formally calculate the ROI of Twitter (even though I probably could), because the value I am receiving is discerned instinctively and is self-regulating. I have precious little time, so I better get something important out of Twitter, if I am going to devote resources to it. Like any investment in time or money, if I don't realize a benefit, I will pull out.

It gets more difficult for a larger business, conditioned to run on data and not on the less-spreadsheet-friendly qualitative benefits that you might be receiving from Twitter and other social media platforms. If the boss doesn't have an appreciation for this, at some point she will wonder what all this Twittering is about and ask for a pie chart. That's when things start to fall apart.

So how do you break the ice? When benefits are difficult to quantify in discrete measures, the best way to explain the value is often through a story.

For most experienced businesspeople, hearing a compelling story of Twitter success can be just as effective as a pie chart. Once somebody understands how the networking operates and the *range* of tangible business benefits that exist beyond just money, it's easy to make the decision to give it a chance. And once they try it, they're usually hooked!

In one case, I was listening to customers tell me how much they were learning from my client's new social media presence. I happened to have my smartphone with me and I asked them if it would be OK for me to take a video of them talking about their observations. When my client saw this powerful feedback, even though it was a crude video—he knew the work we were doing in social media was creating tangible value.

At least that's the way it has worked for me and many of my students and customers. When success doesn't easily fit on a pie chart, sometimes you just have to *show them!*

Another useful tactic is the pilot program. People get nervous about commitment. Ask your boss if you can test it for six months. Then, week by week, pass along the stories as the tangible and intangible benefits accrue. Or, perhaps they won't. Then you can kill the thing gracefully and still get a good performance review!

More Twitter Benefits

I think that, if you follow the guidelines in this book, you *will* see the benefits. No matter your industry or specialty, whether you're a profit or non-profit, whether you work for a Fortune 500 of for yourself, Twitter can absolutely be applied to the business world.

But I still observe many companies stumbling around, debating their return on investment, while their competitors are establishing a social media foothold on a business communication platform that is:

An effective promotional tool[1]—79 percent of Twitter followers (versus 60 percent of Facebook fans) are more likely to recommend brands since becoming a fan or follower. And 67 percent of Twitter followers (versus 51 percent of Facebook fans) are more likely to buy the brands they follow. Daily Twitter users are about three times as likely as Internet users on average to upload photos, four times as likely to blog, three times as likely to post ratings and reviews, and nearly six times as likely to upload articles.[2]

Lead generator—Marketing firm SocialTwist analyzed more than one million links on Facebook and Twitter. Facebook's shared links average only three clicks, while Twitter's tweets generate nineteen clicks on average.[3] Another study showed that, among many small and medium companies, Twitter users generated double the median monthly leads of non-Twitter users. That result held across company size.[4]

Customer satisfier—Service-related companies from appliance manufacturers to the local pizza joint are incorporating Twitter as a cost-effective and popular customer-service connection.

Product development engine—One software company developed an entirely new product line after learning from tweets that people were using their product in new ways. Interesting experiments are emerging to crowd-source innovation through Twitter.

Problem solver—David Sifry, CEO of Technorati, was quoted[5] as saying he used Twitter as a sounding board. "I subscribe to lots of people who say interesting things, and I listen [and] read a lot. I find that these people become a sounding board for ideas, and I learn a lot from them. When I post to Twitter, sometimes it's about interesting things I've seen or observed, and sometimes it's 'questions to the world'—where to find a good consultant for a particular niche specialty—or I ask questions that I can't find easy or reliable answers [to] just by searching Google or reference works."

Using Twitter as a Strategic Weapon

Here's an example of how I realized an exceptional and unexpected benefit from Twitter—developing a PR strategy!

I have a "virtual" company. Well, it's a real company, but I don't have a building and employees and all that traditional stuff. I work with a posse of talented freelancers who may be spread out all over the country. So, I have the best of both worlds. Great company, great people, but no pressure about meeting payroll every month (except my own!).

Everything works great about this model except for one thing. You can't brainstorm by yourself.

This was the problem I was facing recently when I needed to come up with creative ideas to help a client company mark its thirtieth anniversary. I had some ideas, but I've been around long enough to know they weren't the *best* ideas. For that, I needed to put some creative minds together. But how? I was on a tight deadline and needed to write a proposal quickly.

I needed some smart friends that could help me think through this problem in a pinch. And then it dawned on me! That's exactly what I had on Twitter.

This is what the social web is all about—networking, sharing, helping, creating. So, with literally no planning, I sent out one single tweet with an invitation for my Twitter tribe to join me on a web meeting at 4 p.m. that very day.

I was fortunate that seven people were able to join me on the spur of the moment, including one from Brazil and one from Spain. Some I didn't know at all, others had become my friends over months of interaction on Twitter. All were enthusiastic, helpful, and eager to try out this idea of mine!

I used an online service for the actual meeting interface and conference call. To start the meeting, I described the problem and said I was simply looking for a brainstorm of promotional options.

As the ideas were shared, I wrote them out on my shared computer screen, so all participants could build on what was being said. At the end of 30 minutes, I had two pages filled with great ideas. Later that day I massaged the ideas into a proposal, presented it to company management and—ta-da!—they loved it! I had successfully "crowd-sourced" a promotional plan!

There were unexpected side benefits, too:

- I explained to my client how I came up with the ideas, which further strengthened their interest and commitment to the social web.
- The people who connected on the call enjoyed the exercise and have reached out to stay connected with each other.
- I had an idea that worked, that can be repeated, and now shared with you in a book!

Creating a New Product Line

One of the readers of my blog, Fara Hain, described how Twitter search helped her discover an entirely new market for her company's product:

> I admit my initial impression of Twitter was that it was pointless. But it didn't take too long to make me a believer, because I saw first-hand how Twitter helped our company create an entirely new line of business.
>
> While working at Gizmoz [now DigiMe], I was pulled into the world of Twitter by two friends who were early adopters. They encouraged me to try it out, and I started by

"listening" through a daily search for Gizmoz on the Twitter search box. I thought it would be interesting to see what, if anything, people were saying about us. I collated responses into a spreadsheet to see if I could find a theme or locate emerging influencers.

I found that there was a group of people using my site in a completely different way than I had expected. Gizmoz is a B2C 3D animation company that had launched a web-based tool for teens to create greetings and videos using 3D avatars. On Twitter, our tool was being discussed with hashtags like #edtech.

It turns out we were being discussed on the podium at a major education conference! To my surprise, teachers had been using Gizmoz in the classroom as an interactive tool for students to create presentations (science classes, social studies, even a kindergarten class!). We were blown away.

By making some simple changes to our product and asking teachers for their direct feedback, we were able to make Gizmoz more classroom-friendly. We added avatars like Albert Einstein and other historical figures, and we started to be more aggressive about hiding

public posts that featured less appropriate
content.

In our new marketing effort, we actively
targeted teachers—who are, in fact, major
viral influencers—one teacher influencing 30
students is a marketer's dream!

It's doubtful that I would have ever
discovered this amazing new market for our
products without Twitter.

The Power of the Twitter Universe

One last potential business benefit you might not have
considered is the power of the Twitter users to be advocates
for your products and brands.

A study[6] found that consumers active on Twitter are
three times more likely than the average consumer to affect
a brand's online reputation through syndicated Tweets, blog
posts, articles, and product reviews!

The ExactTarget survey of more than 1,500 consumers
concludes that Twitter has become the gathering place for
content creators whose influence spills over into every
other corner of the Internet.

- Twitter users are the *most influential online
  consumers*—more than 70 percent publish blog
  posts at least monthly, 70 percent comment on

blogs, 61 percent write at least one product review monthly, and 61 percent comment on news sites.

- Daily Twitter users are six times more likely to publish articles, five times more likely to post blogs, seven times more likely to post to Wikis, and three times more likely to post product reviews at least monthly, compared to non-Twitter users.

- 11 percent of online consumers read Twitter updates, but do not have a Twitter account themselves!

- 20 percent of consumers indicate they have followed a brand on Twitter in order to interact with the company more than e-mail subscribers or Facebook fans.

And while Twitter is not used as frequently as Facebook or YouTube, an Edison Research study[7] showed that 40 percent of all Americans see tweets or hear about Twitter on a daily basis.

That's why I've spent so much space discussing benefits. Can you really afford to miss out?

Balance. Common sense. Quantitative measurements when you can get them and qualitative measurements when you can't.

Don't let your company miss out on these benefits if traditional measurements don't fit anymore. Don't get caught in analysis paralysis because you can't determine the ROI. To realize these powerful benefits, you need to master the Tao of Twitter, so let's get to it, step-by-step, beginning with those all-important targeted connections.

CHAPTER FIVE

Tao 1: Making Targeted Connections

Many social media pundits and purists would like to have you believe that the quality of your Twitter followers is more important than the quantity. These folks are either naive or liars. In fact, you absolutely need both quality *and* quantity.

Attracting a critical mass of Twitter followers—and by this I mean about 200, in most cases—is very important as you start your journey, for three reasons:

- First, if you have fewer than 200 people who are connecting with you, Twitter is going to be boring. And if it's boring, you're going to quit.
- Second, the more followers you have, the better the chance for a "Go Steelers moment." The more followers, the more potential interactions, the

more interactions, the more opportunities to create business benefits. And we all LOVE those!

- Finally, research published in the journal *First Monday*[1] showed that Twitter users with more followers were more active and more successful.

So, if you are just starting out, I strongly recommend that you spend some time up front working on this critical aspect of your success—even as little as 20 minutes a day for a few weeks can get you started in the right direction.

"If you build it, they will come" makes a great movie line, but a lousy Twitter strategy. There's no shortcut. The only viable and legitimate method to begin to attract targeted followers is to find them, follow them, and hope they follow you back. A rule of thumb is that about 70 percent of the people you follow will follow you back, but there are five simple ideas to tilt the follower odds in your favor.

Five Set-Up Basics

Twitter success starts with setting up your profile correctly. This can easily be accomplished under "settings" on your Twitter home page, which can be found by clicking the "person icon" in the upper right corner of the screen.

When establishing your account, here are some imperatives:

1. Always include a personal photo, preferably a friendly one. No picture = no followers. Trust me. Even if you are tweeting for a company, I would still recommend a photo of a person, rather than a company logo, in most cases. People relate to people, not logos. I'll cover this in much more detail later on.

2. Include a link to your website. After all, you eventually want to drive people there, right? If you don't have a website, direct people to your LinkedIn profile or Facebook page.

3. Create a biography with your business interests that will help people find you in searches. Add some personality! Think about the keywords people would use to find you and your business. Although your bio isn't searchable on the basic Twitter search field (yet), third-party services can use it to help people find you.

4. Choose a short, easy to remember user name, like Sally R. A name like vls767p1 is counterproductive.

5. Even if nobody is following you yet, add a few tweets. People will usually check out your profile and what you have tweeted before deciding to follow you.

Are you ready now? With these profile basics in place, let's start to build an engaged tribe.

Finding Followers

"Following" people is the same thing as adding them as Facebook friends, except that they don't see your updates unless they choose to follow you as well. Generally the best way to get followers is to add people based on your personal interests and business synergies.

Remember that it's not essential for somebody to follow you for you to realize some business benefits. Twitter is a great learning tool; so, if a celebrity, author, industry leader, or professor doesn't follow you back, relax and just enjoy the information they provide. In fact, most people with celebrity status don't follow back.

Once you start following someone, his or her updates, or "tweets," will appear in the "timeline" on your home page. The timeline is just a chronological record of what your followers are saying to you and the rest of the world.

By the way, if you're wondering why the system is limited to 140 characters per tweet, it's because Twitter was built to accommodate being updated from phones. The origin of the 140 character limit is based on the 160 character limit for SMS, which leaves some space for a name in addition to a 140-character message.

22 Ways to Attract Targeted Followers

The first quest of a new Twitter user is to add followers who are interested in the same topics as you. Twitter doesn't really get fun and useful until you have a couple hundred people in your "tribe."

Once you've exhausted your personal and professional contacts, where do you go from there?

Generally, Twitter users follow a rule of reciprocity. If somebody follows you, it is polite to follow him back. Many people are amending this rule over time, as the number of Twitter followers grows, but if somebody shares similar interests, he will probably follow you back—the rule of thumb is that people reciprocate about 70 percent of the time. So a key idea as we get started is to click the "follow" button for some awesome people first, and then hope they will follow you in return. Here are a 22 ideas to build that first targeted audience:

1. Start following people you already know by looking for them on Twitter, using the "Search box" at the top of your Twitter screen. This way you can find existing customers, contacts, friends, and colleagues. Twitter People Search is a very basic *starting point* to find people who may already be on Twitter. If you can't find your friends right away, don't be frustrated. Sometimes they are listed by their handles instead of their proper names.

2. Once you are on Twitter for awhile, you'll notice that people will place you on public "lists." These are generally categorized by a special interest or geographic location. For example, I might be on lists for "marketing experts," "bloggers," or "business educators." If you click on somebody's name and view her profile, you can see every public list she has created and every public list she is on. Dig into these lists, and you will probably find a gold mine of interesting people to follow. List mining can be an addictive activity, as you discover fascinating people and even more lists. Lists are important for many other reasons that we'll cover later.

3. Also look for lists that follow your key stakeholders. For example, if you find a competitor that keeps lists, you might want to check it out and "steal" his followers. All of these lists are public information, so there are no ethical problems with this at all.

4. To take your list investigation to the next level, visit www.Listorious.com, which is a list of Twitter lists. There are hundreds of searchable interest categories to choose from.

5. One of my favorite places to find targeted followers for my clients and students is Twellow.com. This useful little site is like the yellow pages for Twitter. Simply sign in for free with your Twitter information and you're ready to find and follow targeted users. It does not have a complete list of all Twitter users, but it's a pretty good start. Twellow has four useful features:

    a. It has an exhaustive directory of Twitter members by every category, industry, and interest imaginable. Want to find civil engineers? Knitters? Pilots? Dog lovers? They're all here. Results are displayed from the person with the most users to the least.

b. You can also see Twitter users by city, very useful if you only serve a special market.

c. You can search for people by interest *and* city.

d. You can add yourself to up to 10 special interest categories to make it easy for people to find you.

6. Do a Twitter search by your business interests, and follow those who pop up. They will likely look at your profile and become more of your followers. For example, if you are in construction, try searching by:

#construction

#building

#architecture

#remodeling

7. Connect with contacts on Facebook, LinkedIn, and other social media platforms. For example, most LinkedIn accounts now include a Twitter handle. This is a great way of finding people in your industry to follow!

8. Go to TwitterGrader.com. You can find the top Twitter users in a city.

9. Some Twitter applications, like Tweetie and LocalChirps, let you search for posts and tweeters near you by zip code.

10. Another cool third-party application is www .wefollow.com. The user-generated directory has lists of people who associate themselves with particular keywords and interests.

11. Attend Twitter chats based on your industry or interests and follow them. There is more information on chats near the end of this book. These chats are a superb way to find and meet people with similar interests.

12. FilterTweeps allows you to search Twitter bios through various combinations of words, locations, and even by the number of followers they have. This is useful, since people with tens of thousands of followers (a celebrity) may not readily follow you back. Focus on people with fewer than 5,000 followers for the best chance to build relationships, if you are just starting out.

13. Use Twitter's standard "Who to Follow" function on every home page. The algorithm in this feature suggests people you don't currently follow whom you may find interesting. The suggestions are based on several factors, including people you follow and the people they follow.

If you like a suggestion, click "follow," if you don't, click "hide," and it won't suggest that user again.

14. Under "Find friends" you can find Twitter friends by connecting to your e-mail list.

15. Link to your Twitter profile from your other social profiles across the web. On your Facebook page, include a link to your Twitter profile in the websites section. On YouTube, you can link to your Twitter profile in your bio, and in the description section for videos. You can also mention your Twitter username in your videos, or watermark it as text on top of the video. LinkIn has a special field for your Twitter handle.

16. Include your Twitter handle in your e-mail signature and on your business cards.

17. Tweet consistently. To attract Twitter followers, you need to be present. You're not going to attract engaged followers if you only tweet once a month.

18. Create "tweetable moments" in your presentations. When you give a talk to a relevant business audience, include your Twitter handle at the bottom of every slide. One popular speaking tip these days is to actually spoon-feed the audience tidbits they can easily tweet along with your presentation.

19. Traackr is a tool that allows you to find and follow people who are influential in your space. It allows you to identify the "authorities" in your industry who can mean the most to your business or your client's.

20. At the top of the main Twitter home page, you'll see an icon called "Discover." If you click on that, you can see "Activity." This will show new people that your followers are following. There's a good chance these would be good contacts for you, too.

21. Watch whom your followers are recommending and tweeting. Click on their names and see if you want to follow them. In turn, they will probably follow you. "Follow Friday" (covered below) is a great way to find people who might interest you.

22. Twitter has an advanced search function, but, curiously, it is not on the main Twitter site. It's at https://twitter.com/#!/search-advanced. On this site you can find people by keywords and location.

Follower Strategies

Once you begin collecting followers, people will also start finding you. It can be unsettling when people from all over the world start showing up in your list of followers. What do you do about these people?

You'll see two general strategies when it comes to decisions about following people back. There is one group of "celebrities" who might have 50,000 followers, but only follow a few hundred back. Comedian and TV personality Conan O'Brien famously follows only one person!

But if you're not a celebrity (and I'm pretty sure you're not), it's usually a good idea to give people the benefit of the doubt and follow them back. Here's the rule of creating relationships and business benefits through Twitter: *You just never know.*

You never know who will connect with you; you never know how he or she will connect with you; and you never know where it will lead (Go Steelers!).

Having said that, there is a certain element of undesirables, who try to corrupt the conversation by spamming. Twitter does a fairly good job culling these folks but they need our help, too. I go the extra step and "block" people who do not seem to be real people, for four reasons:

1. Your list of followers is public information and reflects on you in some small way. I want an audience to be proud of. This probably sounds old-fashioned, but I don't want to do anything in my life that I wouldn't be proud to disclose to my children. And if they examined my Twitter audience, I would not want them to see a bunch of scantily-clad women peddling their videos. Anybody can see whom you're following. What does your audience say about you?

2. I want to protect my followers. If I block the spamaholics, I keep them from my tweets and I

keep them, in a small way, from my friends. I see
so many of these people who copy "Follow Friday"
lists trying to lure followers in a sneaky way.

3. I just do not want to play that game. I'm not
going to be passive and imply that what they're
doing is OK.

4. Blocking spammers sends a message, and that's
important. But I increasingly believe that having
a quality list of followers, who actually exist
and care about you, is going to make a difference
in social-influence-scoring models, such as
Klout. These systems are becoming important
business tools.

How Many Followers Is Enough?

How many followers you need depends entirely on
your business strategy. As I said, you need a couple
hundred followers for Twitter to start to get interesting,
but remember that you are trying to build a *relevant* and
targeted community. The more people who follow you, the
less real interaction you will have with them, so choose
your "tweeps" carefully.

Let's say you are trying to connect to people who
enjoy single-malt Scotch in a limited geographic area. A few
hundred followers may be all you need. In my business,

I can sell my marketing consulting services literally anywhere in the world, so my potential audience is in the hundreds of thousands of people.

Once you get more than a few hundred followers, you may need a little help keeping up with this wall of noise, and that topic is covered in the "Advanced" section at the end of this book.

A Word About Buying Twitter Followers

There simply is no shortcut to developing an effective, targeted tribe. I recently received this tweet: "Thanks for the follow. I'm gaining daily new targeted followers with www.wyz.com. It's the company everyone uses. Let me know."

While that might sound like a great idea, it's a scam called GFF or Get Followers Fast. No knowledgeable Twitter user would ever use these services. Unfortunately where corruption can occur, corruption *will* occur, and Twitter is no different. There is a cottage industry dedicated to building accounts of blank followers and then selling them to unsuspecting buyers for instant "credibility."

I had a friend call me up and tell me he had just bought a Twitter account and had inherited 6,000 followers. "Now, what do I do next?" he asked.

My reply: "Start over."

There are plenty of scams out there. Avoid them all. Work it the way I've described here and you *will* create business benefits!

CHAPTER SIX

Tao 2: Providing Meaningful Content

When I started using Twitter, I was clueless and frustrated. Sound familiar?

One of the lessons I learned on the path toward Twitter Tao was the power of content—the currency of the social web.

Eager to learn all I could, I was a voracious consumer of free webinars. One session sponsored by the American Marketing Association featured a young entrepreneur named Nathan Egan (@nathanegan), a former LinkedIn executive who had formed a start-up consulting company.

His talk was very interesting—harnessing the power of free web resources to run your company and sales departments more cost-effectively. He hypothesized that the time was coming when you could even run an entire company off of free software and applications.

Nathan seemed like a bright guy, and at the end of the webinar he invited the participants to follow him on Twitter and LinkedIn, so I did.

Through our random posts on Twitter, we began to get to know each other. I was interested in the progress of his company and I apparently appeared on Nathan's radar too, as he began reading my blog, {grow}.

One day, out of the blue, I received a phone call from Nathan. I had just posted to Twitter a new blog article that really resonated with him. "Do you have time to talk for a few minutes?" he asked. "What you wrote reflects my thinking on some things, and I have never really found anybody who understood this topic in this way."

We hit it off and ended up conversing for more than an hour!

Over the next few months, we continued to support each other and share ideas for our respective businesses.

Nathan assembled a great team, and his company grew to the point where he soon needed a wide variety of resources to support projects, and, since I can do a wide variety of things, I seemed to fit the bill! Nathan began sending me paid assignments to fill in the many white spaces of a start-up company.

I loved the work because our views on business and marketing were aligned. As Nathan's trust in me grew, he provided more important, strategic assignments with his

Fortune 500 clients. Eventually, he asked me to be acting Chief Marketing Officer to help him through this exciting growth phase.

As you see from this example, Nathan and I had done a good job of surrounding ourselves with potential business connections—the first step in the Tao of Twitter—but the synergy would not have occurred without some kind of content to grab our attention. Simply hanging out on Twitter or passively observing tweets from others was not going to do it. The catalyst for this connection—and every connection—is *content*.

What was the content that enabled these business benefits?

- The great content on the webinar first introduced Nathan to a group of relevant and targeted people.
- We both tweeted interesting marketing links, ideas, and observations on a regular basis, which kept us on each other's radar screen. We were *present* on Twitter!
- My blog posts through Twitter finally served as a catalyst for live conversations.

Let's explore this idea of providing consistent, compelling content to ignite our new Twitter connections.

A Twitter Content Strategy

The key to turning a faceless follower into a real business relationship is to have a presence on the social web, with relevant and interesting content. When I discussed the strategy of building targeted followers, this covered the *who* of tweeting. Now, we're going to cover the *how, what,* and *when*.

The type of messages you send out will ultimately determine your success and effectiveness on Twitter. If you are interesting, entertaining, and help people with useful information, your followers will be drawn to you and also recommend others to follow you.

If you've never tweeted before, getting started can be difficult, maybe even paralyzing! Sometimes you just get stuck on what to do or say. If you're a newcomer in that category, you might need . . .

A Beginner's Twitter Regimen

Once you get into the tweeting rhythm, it's a lot of fun, but like anything, it takes some practice, and it can be awkward at first. Here are some ideas to help you become a Twitter pro in less than 20 minutes a day.

1. Try tweeting three times a day, at different times of the day. To start, tweet about (a) some interesting non-work-related information you saw, heard,

or read; (b) some news related to your business, market, or industry; or (c) your opinion on something going on in the news or something funny.

2. Check and respond to tweets that mention you and Direct Messages every time you log on.

3. Spend some time reading tweets from the people you follow. Re-sending one of these valuable messages is called a Re-tweet or "RT." Re-tweet somebody at least once a day, and preferably more. Select a very interesting post from somebody, and pass it along to others. Remember to use this format: RT @*follower name* message.

4. If it's Friday, tweet a Follow Friday[1] message for your favorite friends. It might go like this: #FF to these awesome folks: @*followername1* @*followername2* @*followername3*.

When to Tweet

Tweet in the moment. No one is sitting glued to a monitor or smartphone desperately waiting for your next tweet. Twitter, for the most part, is about "the moment." So if something is interesting, timely, and relevant, tweet it.

Tweet at peak times, basically during the day throughout the work week. If your business has international customers across time zones, think about the effectiveness of tweeting at different times of the day or scheduling tweets. Your messages will be more effective if you leave time between your tweets—at least 30 minutes and preferably an hour. If you really want to get into the nitty-gritty details of this, there is a paid application called When To Tweet, and it will show you when your followers are most active on Twitter.

Tweet Regularly. Tweet often, but *only if you have something of value to say.* You should aim for at least a few tweets a day. *Do not have somebody tweet for you*—your followers will eventually figure it out and un-follow you (or worse). Remember, this is about building human, P2P connections.

Scheduling Tweets—Some people like to schedule their tweets to appear at regular intervals, even when they're not at the keyboard. There can be valid business reasons for this. An example would be my friend Aaron Lee (@askaaronlee). Aaron lives and studies in Malaysia, but is trying to build a following of business leaders in North America and Europe. Unless he stays up all night, he probably doesn't have a choice but to schedule his tweets and hope to form new connections in other time zones. He also does an exceptional job following up with people wherever they may be in the world.

What to Tweet

Here is the best, simplest advice I can provide—tweet about what interests you. Although I am a marketing professional and enjoy communicating about that topic, I also love (and tweet about) sports, travel, art, technology, history, science, and many other subjects. I think that helps keep it real and human.

One of the common complaints about Twitter is "I'm not interested in what you had for dinner." Point taken. Still, it is only human—and I think beneficial—to occasionally talk about human stuff—even eating—once in a while, especially as it relates to value-added information, such as a new restaurant or brand you're trying out.

The second most important advice I can provide is to get in a regular habit of sharing. You're already reading much of the day, right? Nearly every newspaper, magazine, blog, and video service allows you to share the content by clicking a tweet button right on the page. When you read something you like, tweet it. It takes no time at all!

Here's a little system that works for me. Over breakfast each morning, I read an electronic copy of the *New York Times*. If I see a particularly fascinating article about a new social media platform, for example, with the push of a button I can "tweet" this article effortlessly to my audience. I have just provided great, interesting content with literally no effort—even while I'm doing something else. Mobile devices can also help you keep on top of content and connected during downtimes.

Finding interesting content is important to attracting and retaining followers. Be sure to mine content from all the sources you might connect with during the day.

- Linking to your blog and other blogs is an obvious source of rich and relevant content.
- Link to comments you create on LinkedIn, Facebook, and other platforms.
- Tweet out an opinion about a special event, something in the news, or a development in your company or community.
- Leverage your other online content. If you have something of value to offer online, like a blog, white paper, or a website, share updates and new posts that you have written.
- Share something human. Did your baby take a first step? Did you close a big deal? Are you grateful for something today? Share it!

The Complete Re-Tweet

Finally, let's spend a little more time on the Mighty Mighty Re-Tweet. There are three important, outstanding benefits of the RT, which simply means re-sharing somebody else's tweet. If you hover over any tweet, you will see an option to Re-Tweet. This is a powerful gesture.

1. It takes the burden of providing all of the content off of you. If you have done a good job surrounding yourself with a targeted audience, they are going to be sharing some great stuff with you. Share it.

2. Sharing another's tweet is a form of a compliment. This is like saying "Great job! I liked this tweet enough to share it." This is a wonderful form of helpful engagement with the person who originated the content.

3. It puts you on the radar screen of the person you tweeted. Really want to get somebody to follow you? Tweet her content a few times and see what happens! She will see each re-tweet in her "mention" column of Twitter.

Here are some bonus ideas to get more mileage from your re-tweets:

Let's say you wanted to re-tweet this tweet from me: @markwschaefer: A key to Twitter success is being authentically helpful.

The standard format would be: RT @markwschaefer: A key to Twitter success is being authentically helpful.

However, the tweet will be read and shared more often if you put the content *first* like this: A key to Twitter success is being authentically helpful. (via @markwschaefer)

Why make your audience work for the content? Put it out there right up front.

To make your tweets more shareable, keep them as short as possible. Every time somebody RTs you, his name is added to the tweet. That 140-character limit is going to be used up pretty quickly so keep it short to begin with.

Snip, Snip, Snip

A URL is the unique name used to identify a website. In fact every piece of content on the web—a post, a video, a photo—has its own descriptor.

The problem is, most of these names are long—quite the problem if you are limited to 140 characters to begin with on a Twitter message! Fortunately, some smart people solved the problem with an application called a URL shortener or "snipper."

When you hit a "tweet button" on an article, the URL is usually shortened automatically. But if you need to shorten a website name, this is easily done with an application such as bit.ly (no "www" just bit.ly). In addition to being a handy little snipper, bit.ly allows you to track how many people actually clicked on your link. This can be highly useful marketing information, if you are trying to determine interest in an announcement, testing different times or methods of tweeting, or if you want to track promotions.

OK, you are one amazing content provider now. But there's still one important aspect of the Tao of Twitter left—authentic helpfulness.

CHAPTER SEVEN
Tao 3: Offering Authentic Helpfulness

When somebody does something great—an interesting blog post, an exceptional insight, a helpful solution—I try to make an effort to compliment him publicly on Twitter. Usually I will just tweet something like "@jfloyd helped me with a problem today. You should definitely follow Jeremy!"

One day I received a tweet from a stranger asking, "We follow each other. Why don't you ever recommend ME?"

My response was: "Because I don't know who you are! Let's change that."

It turns out this stranger was a bright young man named Aaron Killian. I had met him briefly at a speech I gave, but didn't know his name, and we had never connected. Since he lived nearby, I invited him to lunch.

When we met, I discovered that Aaron is a marketing professional with a local United Way. He told me how so many non-profits were struggling in the tough economy, and that meant a lot of needy people were suffering, too. It prompted an idea on how we might work together.

"I've often thought that charities could benefit from using social media tools," I said. "The social web is a great place to tell a story or create emotional connection, and who needs to get more out of their marketing dollars than a non-profit? I've been thinking about an idea to give back to the community. What if I volunteered my time to do some training for the leaders of your charities?"

Of course Aaron was interested in the possibilities, and after some discussions with his president and CEO, we arrived on a concept. I committed to volunteering a full day of social media training to as many people as they could fit in their conference center.

As the day of the seminar grew closer, it occurred to me that this could be an opportunity to create some video content for my business. When I give speeches around the country, it can be difficult and costly to arrange for professional video services. Under controlled conditions in my hometown, I could really save some time and money. I asked Aaron if we could video the session, and he readily agreed. We were able to create two videos, which are on my website today promoting my availability as a business-conference speaker and trainer.

A few days before the event, I tweeted that I was preparing my materials for a seminar for local non-profits.

This information was picked up by a Twitter friend, Tearsa Smith, an anchor for the local TV station. She invited Aaron to a live television appearance on her morning show to promote the event. Twitter is an important source of information and leads for journalists!

The United Way seminar went off without a hitch, but Aaron had to deliver some bad news during the meeting. A local center focused on providing funding to area non-profits had announced it would be closing within the next two months. It appeared that the need to use Twitter and other low-cost social media tools was more important than ever!

The participants were so enthusiastic about my workshop that they proposed meeting every quarter to discuss social media marketing issues. By meeting regularly, they could exchange best practices and look for ways to learn together.

Several of the people decided they loved my ideas so much they wanted to sign up for my college course on social media marketing for business. Not only did they attend, but they also referred others who have now become my students, my friends, and in one case, a new customer!

And, oh yes—Aaron finally got his complimentary tweet!

Have you been keeping a mental checklist of all the benefits that piled up from that single tweet? Quite a few!

So now let's look at the final aspect of the Tao of Twitter—authentic helpfulness. How did it show up in this case study?

- The fact that I was routinely complimenting and supporting other people got Aaron's attention. It made an impact on him, and he wanted to be included.
- We both wanted to meet to get to know each other better.
- By spending the time to meet him for lunch, I was turning an online relationship into an offline relationship. This is a very important part of crystallizing relationships.
- I volunteered my time for the seminar.
- Aaron graciously allowed me to have a video professional record the session to benefit my business.
- Participants continued to help and support each other, both offline and online, following the seminar.
- I subsequently offered advice and support to participants, some of whom later became my students.

There was a theme of helpfulness throughout this story. It was real. Nobody was looking to sell anything to anybody. Aaron wasn't looking to game me—we were authentically supporting each other every step of the way.

A Mindset of Helpfulness

I find many of the social media axioms to be dumb ("It's all about the conversation"—gag me), but here is one that is genuinely useful: Think of the social web as a dinner party. If somebody only talks about himself, his business, and how great he is, you're going to want to get away fast! But if a person shows genuine interest in you, and offers help without regard for his own personal benefit, you will like that person and connect with him.

Like any business relationship, friendships on the social web are built on trust, and that must be earned.

This is the area where most people fail on Twitter, because you can't fake authenticity. If you're only out there to sell, sell, sell, people will sniff you out pretty quickly. Somehow we have lost our way. We've created this digital divide between us and often forget that behind that little Twitter picture is a real, amazing human being who wants to get to know us. Business has always been built on trusting relationships and networking on the web is no different.

Here are some ways to demonstrate true helpfulness to others and engage in a manner that truly builds relationships:

- People throw questions out there all the time.
  Answer them or refer them to somebody who can.

- Build your own tribe. Reach out to the real people on Twitter; don't just kiss up to the most influential ones. Are those folks really going to deliver business benefits to you?
- Read people's profiles. Visit their websites. Read their blogs and comment. You can almost always find something in common with them, and this shows you are genuinely interested. And you should be!
- Nothing says I love you like a re-tweet now and then.
- Check your @ mentions frequently. Make sure you know who is mentioning you and try to respond to him or acknowledge him promptly. Even with a very large following I do my best to personally answer a question or comment directed my way.
- Show gratitude. If someone's helped you out, be sure to thank her publicly.
- Be genuine. Stay honest and let people see your personality.
- Take extended or private conversations to Direct Message (described in the next chapter).
- Use every opportunity to extend the conversation and the relationship by taking it offline. Connect in a deeper way through e-mail, a phone call, or a live meeting.

Being genuine and helpful sounds so easy, doesn't it? But of the three aspects of the Tao of Twitter, this is the one that is most easily overlooked and abused by business professionals trying to fit the old "broadcast" mode of communicating into this new format.

Here is one of my favorite examples of authentic helpfulness in action. About two years ago, I received this e-mail from a complete stranger:

> Mark,
>
> I was inspired by your book *The Tao of Twitter* and wanted to practice authentic helpfulness. I decided to do a few Twitter background pages for you that are based on the feel of your book cover.
>
> I'm happy to make tweaks or revisions, if it's close to what you want but not exactly. Feel free to use or not—it was a fun exercise to try.
>
> Thanks so much for your insights. They reinforced a lot of how I have approached Twitter and provided some new ideas to try.
>
> Carl Brand

Carl, who goes by @MyVogonPoetry on Twitter, has become a friend. I was so moved by this gesture that I wrote a blog post highlighting his act of generosity (while also promoting his business). He has subsequently created a beautiful background for my latest book, *Return On Influence*, and we continue to enjoy each other's company on Twitter. He may also be the funniest man I know! Who knows where it will lead?

Now that we've walked through the three fundamental aspects of the Tao of Twitter, let's put it into action!

CHAPTER EIGHT

Immersion

If you follow the path of targeted connections, meaningful content, and authentic helpfulness, you will have an enormous competitive advantage over those who might take months or years to understand these lessons—if they ever learn them at all.

But even with this knowledge, Twitter can be daunting. It has its own language and vibe. People toss around hashtags and Twitter chats and so many quirky acronyms that it can make your head spin. It can be a bit like entering a foreign country!

In this chapter I'm going to cover some ideas to help you get on the fast track, speed your learning curve, and gain a competitive edge in the Twitter Universe! Let's cover:

- The language of Twitter

- Getting the most from your tweets
- Corrective actions if you fall off track

Let's cut through the clutter one step at a time beginning with . . .

The Language of Twitter

Learning some of the common terms and acronyms is one of the most important things you can do to put yourself at ease. If you're already a Twitter pro, you'll be familiar with the ideas in this section, but if you're new, this is going to help a lot! Here are a few of the most common terms and designations you will encounter:

@ reply—The @ sign is used to indicate that you are replying to a specific username. For example, if your friend Jim Smith tweets a question asking about the best place to buy a Jeep, you will reply with @ JimSmith (or whatever the handle is) "I have one for sale, come on over." Remember that, when you use @reply, it is visible to everyone—even people who don't follow you.

Avatar—The personal image uploaded to your Twitter profile in the Settings tab of your account.

Blocking—The act of blocking keeps a particular Twitter user name from following you and your tweets. You block someone by clicking on his or her profile and choosing "Block" in the settings.

Block and Report—Twitter also gives you the opportunity to block somebody and, if you think he is doing something offensive or illegal, you can also report him to the service. After a few reports like this, he can be suspended from Twitter.

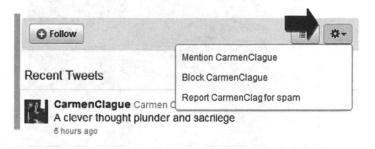

On a profile, the ability to block or report is found by clicking the little settings wheel.

Direct Messages or DM—Twitter equivalent to e-mail. You may only send direct messages to someone you follow and who is also following you. To do this, click on "Message" on her profile and type out your message, again only up to 140 characters. Inexplicably, Twitter has made it somewhat difficult for you to view your own private messages. To find your DMs you have to click the Account icon in the upper right corner and then on DMs.

Feed—Your posts on Twitter are commonly referred to as your "Twitter feed" or "timeline."

Fail Whale—When Twitter is over capacity and unavailable, a cartoon of a whale will appear. So, when Twitter is having technical problems, "whale" jokes are common.

Favorites—Hover over any tweet in your stream, and you will have the option to reply, re-tweet or "favorite," which is symbolized by a star. If you click the star so that it turns yellow, you will save your tweet under "favorites" on your home page. This is a handy tool if you want to come back to something at a later time.

Follow—To follow someone on Twitter means to subscribe to her tweets or updates on the site. You do this by clicking the "follow" button on her profile. Clicking it again will "unfollow" her.

Follow Friday or #FF—It is a tradition to recommend your favorite followers every Friday. This is a polite way of thanking people who have done a good job or did something special to help you during the week. A typical format might be: #FF @user1 @ user2 @user3 for their great content this week!

Hashtags—Hashtags are optional, but useful for denoting groups of tweets to follow. There are four primary uses for the hashtag groupings:

1. Discussions. Some people will designate a hashtag to group all messages from an extended conversation. For example, try doing a search for #blogchat or #journchat in the Twitter search box. You'll find all comments on a certain topic. This figure shows an example of such a search.

 loisgeller If you want to learn some new things about blogging, go to #blogchat next Sunday night.
about 1 hour ago via TweetDeck

 ahynes1 @alisonlaw Thanks for RTing Music Mondays – Blog Mentor, Randy Burns: http://ad.vu/uich You question on #blogchat last night was important
about 2 hours ago via web from Westville, New Haven in reply to alisonlaw

 searchguru @blogworld was a discussion in #blogchat about Wordpress.com deleting my blogs.
about 2 hours ago via TweetDeck in reply to blogworld

 MackCollier @jenniesjursen @mikestenger Point I was trying to illustrate to #blogchat participants was that interacting w others here drives traffic
about 2 hours ago via TweetDeck

2. Topical groupings. If you have a comment you want to show up in a Twitter search, designate it with a hashtag. In this example, the author is indicating that the topic of his tweet is "social media." Therefore, anyone doing a search for this topic on Twitter would find his tweet.

joltsocialmedia Grandma
interviews Brett Greene
http://bit.ly/9RAXzR #socialmedia
28m ago via twitterfeed | Twitter

3. Trending topics. If you want your tweet to refer to a certain news or community event, hashtags can be very useful. For example, during a crisis like the flood in Nashville, citizens could follow news and emergency instructions by simply following #nashvilleflood on their Twitter search.

4. Silliness. People use whimsical hashtags just for fun:

KristenDaukas And now, for my 2,000th tweet, I want to say thanks to all those that I tweet with & learn from on a daily basis. You guys rock. #gratitude
4m ago via HootSuite | Twitter

Locking—You can "lock" your profile so that only friends can see your updates by scrolling down to the bottom of your "Settings" tab on the Twitter website and clicking the box beside "Protect My Updates."

This would certainly deprive you of followers who would have otherwise followed you if they could see your tweets. After all, you're trying to network, right? Since you're reading this book to build business connections, I would strongly recommend that you keep your Twitter feed open and available to anyone who wants to interact with you.

Mentions—Any time somebody uses the @ symbol with your Twitter name (also called handle), it will show up in your list of "mentions," which is displayed if you click the @Connect button at the top of your Twitter home page. This function is extremely important to monitor every day, to see who is mentioning you in his or her tweets. Look for opportunities to engage and help people who are mentioning you by name.

Promoted Tweets—Twitter is finding innovative ways to capitalize on its popularity and monetize its service without impeding users. One way they are doing this is by allowing brands to sponsor tweets and trending topics. Any such tweet or promotion is supposed to be clearly marked as advertising or "promoted."

Recent Images—This is an application on your Twitter profile page that shows recent images you have somehow interacted with—images shared through mobile uploads, images you have tweeted (or re-tweeted from others), images you have commented on, and so forth. Your only option to get these out of your recent images is to delete the tweet associated with the image. You can do this if you click on a recent image and then the Delete link under the tweet.

Re-Tweeting or RT—RT stands for re-tweet, meaning a re-sent message from someone else's Twitter post. If you see RT, this means it is not the sender's original content—it came from the person listed after the RT designation. Another way to credit people for content or a link is to put via @username at the end of the tweet. There are many variations on this theme, but the main point is that it's polite—and good business—to credit others for their good work.

Search—This is located at the top of your Twitter home page. It is a useful tool for finding people,

links, and the latest real-time news. There is also
an advanced search tool and other search tips we'll
cover later on.

Trends or Trending Topics—Located in the left-hand
column of your Twitter home page, this list
indicates the most popular topics in real time. This
is an effective and entertaining way to see what
people are saying about a subject at the moment,
anywhere in the world. You will see tweets
from anybody tweeting on a topic, not just your
followers. Often, the topic at the top of the list is
sponsored.

Tweeps or Tweeples—This refers to a cluster of friends
on Twitter. It is frequently used to address all of
your followers at once, for example, "Morning,
Tweeples!" The Twitter World will try to force
any kind of descriptive word into a format that
begins with "Tw," unfortunately. Another common
example is the . . .

Tweet-up—Twitter folks are very loyal to each other,
and they love to meet in real life (IRL) at social
gatherings called Tweet-ups. Tweet-ups may
be formally scheduled as part of a meeting or
conference or happen on the spur of the moment.
The social side of social media! They can be great
networking events.

Making the Most of Your Tweets

My friend Dr. Ben Hanna led an extensive statistical study to discover the optimal tweeting strategy. Here are four key findings to get the best results from your tweets.[1]

Tweet Quality Versus Tweet Quantity

The study looked at the relative importance of tweeting only when you had something really interesting to pass along (quality focus) versus tweeting more frequently (quantity focus) for building a Twitter following. The study showed that tweet quality is *much* more important than quantity: the higher the average number of clicks per tweet with a trackable link in a given week, the higher the follower growth (controlling for total number of followers). This said, you still have to be in the game; average tweets-per-day over this period ranged from 2.9 to 11.0.

The First Words Are Critical

At 140 characters, tweets are like headlines, and people scan through them quickly. If you want to catch someone's eye, think like a headline writer, and make sure that the main topic keywords or a number/statistic is found in the first three to five words.

The Average Lifespan of a Tweet

If you measure the lifespan of a tweet by the number of days on which it receives at least one click from a Twitter user, then business tweets don't live very long. On average, tweets with a clickable link received at least one click on four separate days, with a range of one day (not a very popular tweet) to 23 days (very popular content).

The Optimal Time Between Tweets

In a study examining the number of clicks on business-related tweets, the optimal space between business tweets to attract the most clicks is either 31–60 minutes or 2–3 hours. Tightly packed tweets just don't appear to attract as much attention as tweets with more space between them. The cause of the dip in click activity for tweets between 61 and 120 minutes is uncertain.

If You Get off Track

Research shows 60 percent of those who try Twitter quit in the first week. Hey, I was one of them! It can be an incredibly frustrating experience, especially if you're trying to build momentum in a corporate environment. If you start spinning your wheels, here are a few strategies to get back on track.

Be Tenacious

Twitter is a viable business communication channel, end of story. "From what I've determined in our research, Twitter has a role as a business communication channel for most companies," Dr. Hanna said. "If you've already tried Twitter for your organization and struggled to make it work, it's most likely because the social media rules for your industry and customers are still being written. Don't give up."

Twitter as Mass Communication Versus Personal Communication

Maybe you feel like you're not connecting with followers as you should. Perhaps it's time to review your fundamental communication strategy. Conventional wisdom among many Twitter-advocates is that you are building a "community." Certainly that can be true on a personal level, and even for small organizations, but it's not necessarily feasible for large businesses. Some very large brands now have "war rooms" following social media feeds from around the world and teams of full-time tweeters. The good news is, it's easy to experiment to find the right rhythm and scale for your business.

Is Anybody Home?

If you are using the tools I've described to identify your list of meaningful connections and still can't find potential customers, maybe you need to review your strategy and underlying assumptions. Are your customers using social media? If so, which ones? If not, are you in a position to lead and establish a point of competitive differentiation? The nature of business communications is changing so rapidly, don't assume you really know your customers right now, especially if you don't see them often!

Focus on Quality

You already know that tweeting interesting things has a much bigger, more positive influence on follower growth rate than tweet volume. This holds true for businesses too. Blanketing your followers with tweets doesn't work any better than blanketing the media with press releases, or hammering a direct mail list with irrelevant offers. Here's a best practice idea for businesses: Remember our little snipping tool friend bit.ly? Well, this application will show you how many people are clicking on your links, essentially "grading" your effectiveness. Experiment to find content and sources your customers like best.

Tao Times Two

I've taught social media marketing classes to hundreds of business professionals, and sometimes it just doesn't "take" the first time. Maybe the timing wasn't right or they had other priorities at the time. Maybe the incentive didn't seem to be enough for them to commit. Perhaps the first go-around of information was just too overwhelming. But usually everyone comes around. If you find yourself lagging behind, scan this book again, especially the first few chapters explaining Connections + Content + Helpfulness and the business benefits.

Be Patient

It might take months, or even longer, to realize business
benefits from Twitter, depending on your devotion to
the channel and your objectives. In any event, it does
take time, and that fact doesn't go down easy for many
impatient business owners. Follow the Tao of Twitter.
It will happen.

CHAPTER NINE

Lists—The Key to Twitter Sanity

Once you get more than a few hundred followers, you're going to need some help wading through the noise. Twitter Lists will help keep you organized and tuned in.

As you get into the flow of Twitter, you'll probably find yourself naturally grouping people in your mind. Customers. Competitors. My online friends. People I admire.

Twitter Lists allow you to organize the Twitter stream so you can make sense of what might seem like chaos.

By clicking on the main account icon and then the word "Lists," you'll be on your way to using this essential utility for monitoring the tweets from smaller groups of people who are important to you. You can make the Lists public for the world to see, or keep them private.

If you see Lists from others that you like, you can "follow" an entire List. Likewise, others can follow your lists. Some people are even making a business out of curating important and popular Lists.

Eventually, you'll probably want to export your Twitter Lists to a third-party application called a "listening deck." More on that later.

Lists are very important as a personal productivity tool, but they are also important to businesses in many ways. I've already discussed their crucial role in finding targeted followers. Here are some additional ideas to leverage your public lists in creative ways.[1]

Share Your Lists on Other Platforms

Most people share their lists within Twitter. But don't stop there. Plan on sharing the links to your lists on your website or blog. Lists will be accessed via a URL like this: http://twitter.com/user_name/list_name. To promote the list on your website, you'll just add a link with the URL. Why not share them on Facebook, in e-mail, and through your newsletter?

Include Yourself in Your Lists

Since people can subscribe to your Lists, be sure to include yourself, so they can see your tweets. As people follow these lists, they will be following you, too.

Name Your Lists Well

You'll give your Lists names, and those names will be part of the shareable URL. Choose a name that is enticing and accurate such as "my favorite bloggers" or "metals industry experts."

Create Lists Helpful to Your Target Audience

Think of Lists as a marketing tool. Ask yourself these questions (bloggers, replace "customer" with "audience"):

- Who are my target customers?
- Do they fall into distinct segments with different needs or interests? If so, define each customer segment.

- What are their goals, as they relate to my area of business?
- What kind of information helps them reach those goals?
- What kind of information is this type of customer generally interested in?
- Who on Twitter regularly tweets that kind of information?
- What Twitter resources can be valuable to this customer segment, given their goals?

Now, using the answers to that last question, create one or more Lists for each customer segment, designed to meet their goals. For example, let's say you're a Realtor. You'd like to attract potential home buyers in the Chicago area. You might decide that the key customers you want to attract are first-time home buyers and people thinking of selling. You come up with this list of information goals for first-time buyers:

- Information about the home-buying process
- Information about mortgage types, qualifying, and so on
- Tips for home-shopping
- Information about what to look for in walk-throughs, inspections, and so on
- How to decide what you want in a house

- Information about neighborhoods, amenities, schools, and so on
- Real estate market and interest rate trends

Based on this List, you're able to find several bloggers and home magazines on Twitter that tweet about home buying, loan types, the home buying process, and so on. You find some good Twitter sources for mortgage and interest-rate information. You find several Twitterers who tweet about Chicago neighborhood statistics or tweet links to articles and blog posts about neighborhoods, and so on. And you add all of these sources, and yourself of course, to create your Chicago First-Time Home-Buyer List.

Remember, these Lists can also be followed by competitors! Be aware of the competitive environment.

Use Lists to Create Mini-Communities

Let's say you blog about parenthood, or you're a retailer that sells products for new and expecting parents. *Why not build a community that also aligns with your business needs?*

Create a list for expectant parents on Twitter. Make the initial list from whomever you know who is expecting, then invite others to join your list. Spread your invitation far and wide on Twitter, your site, Facebook, and so on. Expectant parents can send a message to you to get added to the list.

Ask the List members to nominate other expectant parents on Twitter. Keep spreading the word until you hit the 500 List-member limit.

Now, you've created a mini-community consisting of your target market. It's a great resource for the List members and provides a real service to them. It's a place they can go to view the tweets of other expectant parents, kind of like a chat room. In the process, you've met a whole bunch of new potential customers that you can now get to know and share your products with.

Well, by now I hope you're starting to get a little more comfortable and confident in the language and workings of the Twitter platform. And of course you're constantly working on your Tao: connections, content, and helpfulness. Now, let's see how these ideas can be applied for specific business marketing initiatives.

CHAPTER TEN

20 Ideas to Toast Your Competition

Let's start putting some of these ideas to practical use for your business or organization. In fact, Twitter can be a powerful competitive advantage for many people!

Just because we're talking about marketing and competition, don't think I'm going to let you forget the "social" part of social media. Whether you work at a small business, a giant corporation, or a non-profit, I'd like you to take a Post-it Note and put this on your computer:

Social media is P2P

Person to person. This is the heart of our Tao, isn't it? If you take one thing from this book—and it is the one thing most businesses disregard—remember that you are connecting to real people, not avatars. Business is built on relationships, and you are only working toward that end if you keep "P2P," not "press release," at the top of your mind.

There are lots of success stories and case studies documenting business success through Twitter. Here are a few of my favorite ways to leverage this platform for new business benefits.

1. Listen Up! Twitter is a source of hugely valuable information for businesses. Its public nature and real-time status allows business users to research topics, follow market conditions, locate and learn about clients and their employees, follow relevant news, and much more. The scope for businesses using Twitter is enormous, from insurance companies being able to understand the day-to-day lifestyles of prospective life insurance candidates, to employers tracking which recruitment candidates are most suitable for their company, and even account managers using client timelines as a source of information to enhance relationships.

Twitter as a tool for listening is frequently the first port of call for businesses choosing to embrace Twitter. Listening doesn't require action, or even a Twitter account, which makes it a relatively safe approach to the platform.

2. Customer service. What's the world's favorite Twitter activity? Complaining! Which is fine, unless the complaint is about you or your company! Digging deeper into Twitter, listening can mean far more than monitoring the frequency with which a keyword is used, instead offering businesses the ability to augment their customer-support offerings with a relatively low-cost tool. Major businesses, including AT&T and Microsoft, now run a significant part of both their B2B and B2C customer service functions through social media, with Twitter taking a central role. Advanced tools can also immediately rate the sentiment of complaints and the relative online influence of the person complaining.

Addressing customer-service issues in the public eye using an inherently visible platform such as Twitter is a bold move for the companies taking this approach. However, it is ultimately rewarding, as customers can see a commitment to quality products and services associated with the decision to use social media in this manner.

In a legendary Twitter story, well-known blogger Heather Armstrong, who had just purchased a new washing machine to keep up with the diapers of her prodigiously pooping newborn, discovered that her $1,300 appliance didn't work. After several weeks of botched service calls, Heather vents on Twitter: "So that you may not have to suffer like we have: DO NOT EVER BUY A MAYTAG. I repeat: OUR MAYTAG EXPERIENCE HAS BEEN A NIGHTMARE."

After a few similarly-scalding messages, the magic began. She received messages from Maytag competitors offering help. Then she received a phone call from an executive at the Maytag corporate office, who contacted an alternate repair service, had the appropriate parts over-nighted, and had the machine repaired in less than a day. And competitor Bosch offered to give her a free washing machine, which she accepted and donated to a local shelter.

Most businesses MUST be listening on Twitter!

3. Twitter can be an incredibly powerful way to conduct business intelligence:

- Follow your competitor's Twitter stream.
- Monitor their replies (save a search on Twitter).
- Analyze their followers.
- Watch for their customer interactions and announcements.
- Monitor their score on Klout.com as a measure of their social media effectiveness.

4. Discover consumer problems, product issues, or potentially damaging PR disasters by picking up conversations about your company and responding quickly. A friend of mine in Canada actually specializes in this—monitoring the social buzz for impending strikes or disturbed company employees.

5. Break through communication barriers with tweets. Having a hard time making that business connection with a new lead through cold calls and e-mail? Try a tweet or direct message. You will not believe how well this works. They may not return your calls, but they almost always return tweets! I don't know the psychology behind this. I only know it works!

6. Run special deals and promotions on Twitter that you can use to drive traffic or move slow-moving stock. If you've done a good job surrounding yourself with targeted connections, they should be interested in your specials, right? A local bakery is using this idea to move their products quickly if they've baked too much of a certain item that day "come by before 4 p.m. for 2-for-1 coffee cakes." Hey, coffee cakes would certainly be meaningful content in my estimation! Especially cinnamon.

7. Twitter is an exceptional way to build your personal brand beyond your normal business borders. Even if you travel constantly, the opportunity for global reach through Twitter probably has more potential, with a lot less wear and tear.

8. Find new business contacts and sales leads through directories such as Twellow and the advanced Twitter search. We earlier discussed the concept of "pre-populating" new business relationships as a powerful networking advantage.

9. Did you know Twitter can help your visibility on search engines such as Google? Just a few years ago, search results would only turn up websites. Now you're just as likely to get LinkedIn profiles, video, and, yes, Twitter profiles—and even individual tweets. The "social" component of search is becoming increasingly important to platforms such as Google and Bing.

10. Use your tweets as real-time testimonies. Tweets are published and permanent, so feel free to use them as marketing tools. An example: One college featured real tweets about their school on an electronic highway billboard (not in real time of course!). A coffee shop featured happy customer tweets on a flat-screen display in their shop.

11. Public validation. As people send compliments and nice tweets about you, save them in your "favorite" Twitter function. When you need to pull out some "social validation," simply direct them to your Twitter page or the link to your "favorites." This is public information for all to see.

12. The PR opportunities are significant. Journalists are extremely active on Twitter, seeking information on story leads and sources. You might get some unexpected PR placements if you establish yourself as a voice of authority on Twitter, especially if you combine this with blogging. Consider creating a list of your local media professionals and look for opportunities to network as you follow their stream.

13. I love the way businesses are using Tweet-ups— networking meetings of Twitter enthusiasts—to effectively promote their organizations. Twitter loyalists love to get together to meet in real life—especially if there is free food involved! If you have an appropriate meeting space or venue, why not sponsor a Tweet-up to introduce folks to your facility while giving them a friendly place to meet? I think this would be effective for restaurants and clubs, banks, non-profits, schools, health clubs, real estate offices—almost any place with a large meeting space that serves local clients.

14. Twitter is a great way to keep up on the latest news and trends. What if you turned this into a competitive weapon for your entire organization? What would be the implications, if your employees had access to real-time news and market information that your competitors didn't have?

15. In a little while, I'll cover Twitter Chats in depth. But if your industry does not already have one, creating your own public chat can provide some competitive advantage, as you connect to people specifically interested in you and your chat topics.

16. Twitter is an excellent way to establish thought leadership for your brand in your community, especially if respected company executives are active on the site. The aim is to establish a leadership position in a particular field by creating and sharing content around a particular topic, as well as passing on opinions or statements on curated content. Many senior executives practice this approach, using a personal account on behalf of a company.

17. Connect through a funny persona. A few companies have successfully created funny and entertaining anonymous personas behind their brand. A Taco restaurant in the Pacific Northwest makes wisecracks about its

Mexi-fries. The fashion brand DKNY had an anonymous tweeter for years giving entertaining insights into the fashion world. Creating interest through funny alter egos is risky business but if you have the right personality, it can work in some circumstances.

18. Through Twitter, offer helpful links and headlines that can drive traffic to your website, blog, landing pages, YouTube channels, Facebook page, and so on. Despite the social media hype, your website is usually the place where you actually ask for money, or registrations, downloads, uploads, or whatever you're after. Websites are still important in the social information ecosystem.

19. Build loyalty. In my experience, the Twitter community is fiercely loyal to its active members. One local business person asked me if I knew of an accountant on Twitter, she wanted to do business and reward somebody active in the local social media community if possible. Many towns now have Social Media Clubs where you can meet other business professionals on Twitter and build those off line connections.

20. And one last business idea—something NOT to do. Do NOT put a Twitter feed on your website. Yes, it's cool. Yes, it's trendy. But it can backfire on you.

Done correctly, Twitter is lively, personal, and human. If you display your Twitter feed on your website, you're displaying one side of a two-sided conversation. It's conversation out of context. Why would you do this? What possible value could this create?

A couple years ago, a friend asked me to review his website. When I went to his landing page the thing that hit you right in the face was the word "PORNOGRAPHY" in the Twitter stream. In context, he was making a funny comment in response to a friend. On a website it sends the wrong message.

Everything communicates. Everything you say, and everything you don't say, reflects on your brand. "LOL!!!! You rock Tony!" and "Delayed in Dallas for the second time this week" are appropriate for a Twitter stream, but is that the kind of business communication you want to display on your company website?

Of course if your Twitter stream is simply company links and press releases you're safe. But you're also probably not too successful on Twitter.

The only possible value there could be is some symbol of social validation, like "Hey everybody, look at us! We're on Twitter." That just seems kind of desperate. If you provide value on your blog or website, why wouldn't a person want to follow your social stream anyway?

Meanwhile, this widget is taking up valuable real estate that could be better used to create a call to action, promote a product or service, or offer something legitimately helpful.

So there you have it. A few of my favorite business applications for Twitter. I know you're probably so excited to try some of these new ideas out that you can hardly wait to finish the book!

But wait a minute . . . what's that loud vacuuming sound I hear? Why, it's Twitter sucking all your time away! This is a reality you're going to face all too soon. Twitter can take a ton of time, and it can also be fun and addictive. So let's tackle the issue head-on by providing a few actionable ideas to keep this thing under control.

CHAPTER ELEVEN
Twitter Time Savers

"How much time should I spend on Twitter?" is a question I get asked repeatedly.

There's no absolute answer to that question, just as there is no good answer to how much money a company should spend on advertising or how many resources should be devoted to research and development. It is completely dependent on your goals and the competitive structure of your business.

The time needed to do social media marketing right is a significant obstacle for many organizations. Part of the reason for this is that the duties are frequently piled on top of already-full plates at work. That's not fair, it's not smart, and it's not going to work as a long-term strategy.

Instead I'd like to have you rethink your entire approach to marketing and how new social media channels like Twitter fit in. Your customers are probably spending more time on social networking sites and less time on e-mail, trade shows, and journals. Even views of most traditional websites are down in the past few years. Maybe it's time to re-think how you split up your entire budget and the time you're spending with traditional media and other networking channels.

When I started my own business many years ago, I devoted an enormous amount of time and expense to live networking meetings. You know the type. Chamber of Commerce meetings. Networking "speed dating." Trade shows. Business Networking International.

At the time I started my business, this seemed to be the only alternative. My last "corporate" job was global in nature. For years I had been leading teams in China, Russia, Brazil, Australia—almost every corner of the world—and really had no significant business connections in my own region of the country! So I had to get out and press the flesh.

I dutifully began the circuit of lunch and breakfast meetings, hoping beyond hope that a connection would lead to a connection and conversations would turn into customers. It was an endless loop of meeting the same insurance salespeople, bug exterminators, and Realtors over and over again.

Then came the moment that made me realize I *had* to find another way. I attended a local networking meeting called "TNT." I can't remember what it stood for, but I'm pretty sure the middle word was "Networking." At the beginning of the meeting, everybody stood up and said something nice about his or her business. At the end of each uplifting description, the whole room yelled "BOOM!" TNT—get it? I didn't know it was coming, and after that first BOOM somebody had to peel me off the ceiling.

This just wasn't for me. And it wasn't working anyway. Sure, I met lots of nice people, but they were all trying to sell something to *me*, too. I acquired a few small local customers, but they were not prepared to think and work on the strategic level I enjoyed. They needed yard signs, not company strategies. If I stuck with it, I could have made a living, but I needed to paint on a much bigger canvas.

And these meetings were taking up too much valuable *time*. Some of the events were lasting an hour and half or more every week, plus travel time. When I discovered Twitter, I realized that I could connect with highly-targeted individuals instead of taking potluck each week. And I could cast my net more broadly—globally, in fact—without ever leaving my office. I could connect on my time, my terms, and my schedule. In my pajamas.

As the enormous benefits of Twitter networking accumulated, I stopped the time-consuming and expensive local meetings completely. Today, I have a thriving international business, built almost entirely through social networking. My four largest customers, five most important collaborators, and my teaching position at Rutgers University all came to me via Twitter connections.

Now don't misunderstand. I'm not saying there is no value to live networking. Of course there are powerful benefits for many people, and there always will be. I'm only saying that for *my individual strategy,* online networking became a more effective source for qualified leads and business value. My point is, I could spend more than an hour a day on Twitter and it would still save me time compared to what I was doing before. It's something to think about.

So how much time does it take? If you're just starting out, let me suggest you put a stake in the ground and devote at least 20 minutes a day. Chances are, you will want to spend more time than this, but let's start there.

I've divided this chapter into two categories—how you should spend 20 minutes a day as a beginner, and then the same approach for more experienced Twitterati.

The 20-Minute Regimen for Beginners

In a world focused on "engagement" and "conversation," I'm going to give some unconventional advice: Forget about it for a few weeks. If you're a beginner and can only spend 20 minutes a day on Twitter, concentrate on Tao Lesson Number One: Building a relevant tribe of followers for the reasons we've already covered.

So, in the first two months, tweet at least once a day, so people see that you're active, but spend most of your time finding and following interesting people using the techniques discussed in Chapter 5. Don't worry if people follow back or not. That will come in time. Building an engaged, meaningful tribe is the prerequisite to any future success.

Now for the other half of your time, spend it reading, and occasionally responding to, tweets from your new friends. This will give you the chance to see what kind of tweets you like, which is instructive when you start tweeting more heavily yourself. This will also begin to get you in the rhythm of Twitter and on your way to creating fascinating new relationships.

The 20-Minute Challenge for Pros

Let's face it, if you're really immersed in Twitter, the challenge is probably how to not spend *all* your time on this addictive little channel! Once you have surrounded yourself with interesting people, it's easy to "go down the rabbit hole" and follow link after fascinating link.

Now that you have built up a critical mass of at least 200 followers, it's time to take advantage of this amazing resource and engage and build meaningful connections, the second lesson of Tao. Here are a few time-saving corner-cutters:

- Get in the habit of sharing on Twitter every time you're reading on the Internet. A handy tool like Buffer can help you fan out your tweets throughout the day if you are coming across many interesting items of content at one time.

- If you're only spending 20 minutes a day on Twitter, do it at different times of the day, so you have the chance to interact with a broader range of people.

- In the next chapter I'll discuss powerful organizing tools, such as TweetDeck or HootSuite. These are excellent platforms to improve your efficiency by helping you focus on those who are actively connecting with you.

- One of the most time-efficient Twitter strategies is to look for opportunities to re-tweet posts. This covers two bases at one time—you're providing interesting and meaningful content and connecting with a follower, too.

- Use a utility such as Ping.fm to post information on Twitter, Facebook, LinkedIn, and other platforms simultaneously.

- Another great time saver is using a Twitter application for a smartphone. Use those idle minutes waiting to pick up the kids at school!

Can you keep up with everything going on in your Twitter stream? No way. Not even if you spent 10 hours a day! Being effective in 20 minutes a day means knowing how to use these time-saving tips and then having the discipline to prioritize.

If you are in a business like selling personal services, or you have a business that can benefit from a lot of personal networking, you will want to spend increasing amounts of time on this communication channel as the payoff begins to be realized.

Out-Sourcing: The Ultimate Time-Saver?

Can you out-source your tweeting to an advertising or PR agency? Perhaps that would be the ultimate time-saving measure?

You should always strive to be genuine on Twitter, as with all other marketing activity, and if you are creating a personal profile attached to an individual, then that individual should always do their own tweets. Period.

I have a friend who had been building a Twitter relationship with a business executive she admired. They had tweeted back and forth a few times and he had provided some helpful career advice to her. When they had a chance to finally meet at a networking event, she introduced herself and was met with a puzzled stare. He had never heard of her before, and sheepishly explained that his PR agency was tweeting for him. Obviously his reputation was ruined for this young woman . . . and also to all those she talked to about the incident!

In a well-publicized snafu, a PR agency rep tweeting on behalf of Chrysler Corporation sent out this tweet: "I find it ironic that Detroit is known as the motor city when no one here knows how to f**cking drive."

He thought he was tweeting from his personal account, but in fact, it came from Chrysler's Twitter account by mistake. He lost his job, and the agency lost the account.

Faking it on Twitter is dangerous business.

But if you are in a situation where you have no other practical choice than to "team-tweet" behind a brand name, then you could outsource or share the tweeting between a few trusted individuals. If you do outsource:

- Be clear and realistic on your objectives.
- Have clear lines of who owns what.
- Have a clear plan for content, tone, and frequency.
- Be prepared to take advice and listen to it. Most experts know what they are doing, and it's in their best interests to make it work for you.

Make sure that you have a disaster recovery plan in case of a PR upset. If you're using an agency, ask them to show you how they are managing your account distinctly from personal/other client accounts, so that tweets aren't mistakenly sent from the wrong account—easy to do when you're using a shared platform. Ask to meet everyone who will be tweeting via your account and create some rules or guidelines for tweeting. Outsourcing doesn't mean abdicating responsibility—make sure you are involved and holding everyone to account.

Before you outsource, carefully weigh the risks and benefits. One of the biggest opportunities of social media is "humanizing" the brand, and even the biggest brands are finding ways to do that successfully. In the long term, businesses should aim at involving their own employees to be "brand beacons" on Twitter instead of relying on an outside agency.

CHAPTER TWELVE

Balancing the Personal and the Professional

What is the proper balance between personal and professional outreach on Twitter? If you are using an account to promote company and client content, is it also appropriate to carry on conversations on a personal level about sports, a great recipe, or my favorite charity? Do we need to have *two accounts*?

This is a great question and one that I have to address on two levels, the philosophical and the practical.

At its heart, Twitter is a business networking tool . . . which is what many companies and individuals don't understand. They view the platform as just another way to broadcast company advertising and press releases. By trying to force-fit old "broadcast" media thinking into this new platform, they are, at best, sub-optimizing Twitter, and, at worst, hurting their brands.

Think of yourself in another networking situation . . . say an industry conference or a chamber of commerce meeting. Would you stand there and read press releases? No, of course not. You would seek out great people to connect with, discuss subjects that are interesting to you and them, and look for ways to work together. Twitter can work exactly the same way.

So even if you are playing a business "role" on Twitter, there is no reason you can't be yourself, unless you are a naturally mean and sucky person. If you are in that category, you either have to not be mean and sucky or not use Twitter. And if you are truly, chronically mean and sucky, you probably will fail at business anyway, let alone at Twitter, so it's better that you find out sooner than later, I suppose.

When networking, the most powerful relationships are built on trust and friendship, so it's OK to let people know a little bit more about what is going on in your life, including your love of sports, charity, family, or whatever is happening around you. As you go throughout your day, just tweet what is interesting to you, as long it is appropriate and professional.

In most cases, I do not think it makes sense to have both a personal and a business account. You're not two people, and being yourself is not only a great way to build your business network, it humanizes your company brand.

OK, now I'll get off my soapbox and examine some practical realities. Even if you have this concept down, maybe your company doesn't. If your job is to be your official company Twitterer, you probably have marching orders to follow a role or social media policy that has you tweeting behind a logo. You might even have a (gasp) script. Here's what you should do in that case: Follow the company policy. Don't lose your job over Twitter. You can still work to change attitudes over time.

There are several compromises or hybrid strategies to blending personal and professional approaches on Twitter. Here are the four types of organizational Twitter accounts. Which one fits for you?

All Business, All the Time

In rare cases it is entirely appropriate to "broadcast" over Twitter. Here's an example: Citi has a site that only broadcasts job openings. They really don't need to engage in a conversation, and they're not even trying to. Notice that they follow nobody. They have jobs, people want them, and they subscribe to the account. It's that simple. They could probably work to build a community, but why?

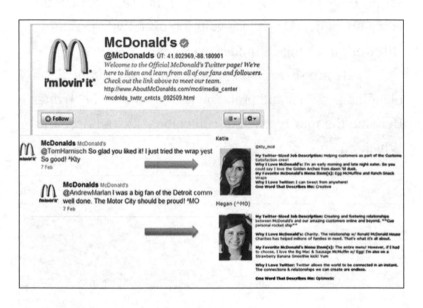

Tweeting Under Cover

Many of the world's most important brands have teams of tweeters engaging with the public behind corporate logos. In the example of McDonald's Twitter account, the initials of the tweeter show up at the end of each tweet and following a link in the Twitter bio leads you back to profiles of the individuals providing the tweets. Certainly a great option to humanize the brand and still operate under one brand banner.

Blending the Personal and the Corporate

In some cases, there is a corporate account assigned to an individual. When that person moves on, the profile is still owned by the company. One example of this is @sharpiesusan, who tweets on behalf of Sharpie pens. Susan has built up a faithful following, but when she moves on to another job someday, this brand equity will stay with the parent company Newell-Rubbermaid, and Susan will simply be replaced.

This also works well in a customer-service situation. In the example above, ATT has accounts set up for the representatives that can be moved over to other representatives as they change and take on new roles. So the connection is human, but the role can be interchangeable.

Real People in Real Time

Usually the best option is to have real people representing your company, like my friend Chad Parizman, representing Scripps Networks in the example. The ultimate goal for a company is to get to a place where many employees can serve as beacons for your brand. He tweets as himself but is cognizant that he is always "on" for his company.

Over a period of years, I became friends with a fellow in London who works in IT for a huge global consulting firm. When he learned that I was coming to the U.K. on a business trip, he introduced me to his company's marketing leadership, and I ended up conducting a very successful social-media workshop for the company. I didn't get connected to this company through the normal channels. In fact, the whole event was planned without a phone call. To me, my IT friend *was the face of this company,* and this resulted in concrete business benefits for his firm.

Wouldn't it be amazing to use Twitter in this way to unleash the power of every person in your organization as a potential salesperson?

CHAPTER THIRTEEN
Secrets of Influence on Twitter

The notion of "influence" is among the most debated and emotional topics you can bring up among the social media crowd. Even trying to *define* influence will invite an argument! At the end of the day, as long as you are satisfied with the business benefits you're receiving from Twitter, what anybody else thinks is irrelevant.

Still, whether you're a business professional or simply an enthusiastic participant on the social web, we should all be aware of this increasingly important trend of social influence and consider how it might affect our opportunities.

While you may abhor the idea of a company like Klout judging or grading you on a daily basis, it's already happening and companies are paying attention, so we shouldn't just ignore this trend.

Dozens of "social influence" scoring themes have emerged, and they are already being used by major corporations to identify thought leaders and create new marketing initiatives.

If you're particularly interested in this subject, you would probably enjoy the best-selling book *Return on Influence: The Revolutionary Power of Klout, Social Scoring, and Influence* by one of my favorite authors. Me!

But let's look at a few Twitter-specific ideas to consider. All of these scoring systems keep their computations closely held—that's their secret sauce—so you will never read a definitive theory on how to improve your scores across the board. The factors are too different and ever-changing. One executive insider told me his company tweaks his formula every single day.

Like most approaches to the dizzying world of social media, the strategy for improving social influence is to focus on the basics that are under your control. And that leads us back to the path described in this book, *The Tao of Twitter*. Let's look at how your focus on connections, content, and helpfulness will improve your chances for a more effective "social imprint" on any grading system.

Targeted Connections and Social Influence

Every scoring system has some accounting for the number of followers, the "quality" of your followers, or both.

The fundamental follower strategies defined in this book should support these factors of influence. Using some of the techniques I've discussed, spend time building a targeted, relevant audience. While some pundits will tell you numbers don't matter, I've already shown you that they do. More relevant connections = more opportunities for business benefits.

Remember to cull your followers by blocking obvious spammers. Why does this have such an important impact on social scoring?

Let's say I have 250 Twitter followers in my targeted and relevant audience. These people are more likely to engage with me through tweets, re-tweets, and recommendations to others than are spammers who are only interested in building lists or broadcasting get-rich-quick schemes.

For example, if I send out a tweet and it's re-tweeted or commented on by 15 people, that's an engagement ratio of 6 percent.

Now let's say Mr. Bigshot Twitter King has 10,000 followers, but only half of them are even real people. He never bothered to look at who is following him and is more interested in the appearance of a large number of followers. If he sends out the same tweet that I do, it may attract some form of engagement from 50 people. Wow, that seems like it generated a lot of influence compared to 15 in the first example!

But let's look a little more closely. Considering his large number of followers, Mr. Bigshot Twitter King had an engagement ratio of only .05 percent. On a percentage basis, he had less influence on his audience, because most of followers aren't even real. By most social influence systems, he would receive less credit over time for this level of influence!

Taking the time to nurture and curate a quality list of followers takes extra effort, but in the long run it will provide benefits in terms of social influence.

You need both quality engagement and quantity of followers to ultimately be successful.

Meaningful Content and Social Influence

The core measure of most scoring systems is an ability to show how many people react to your tweets and how often.

That means you better be tweeting out something special! Providing consistent and compelling content is an important factor in the social influence formulas. Can you see how this goes hand in hand with focusing on a targeted and relevant community? If you surround yourself with people likely to be interested in you, they're going to be more likely to engage with you and share your content. The more they share and react to your content, the more you are demonstrating to these scoring systems that you are influential.

Remember our little friend bit.ly, the helpful tool to "snip" URLs? Here's a trick to also let it help you measure and increase the level of engagement you receive.

One of the advantages of bit.ly is that it saves all of your links and displays how many times those links were clicked (even by time of day). It's almost like observing your audience voting on your content.

By doing a few experiments with different types of content at different times of the day and different days of the week, you might see a pattern of content that is the most popular.

After you've been on Twitter for awhile, you will certainly get an intuition about what content generates engagement by the instantaneous feedback of replies and re-tweets.

Authentic Helpfulness and Social Influence

Another aspect of social influence is *who* is engaging with you. If you are influencing the influencers . . . well, you would be more influential! That sentence might make you a little dizzy, but I think it makes sense, right?

This can be a tricky business. How do you get busy people—maybe even those with a bit of celebrity ego—to even follow you, let alone engage with you?

The answer comes through your conscientious efforts to be helpful. If you're helpful, kind, informative, and useful, you'll be much more likely to appear on somebody's radar screen.

You might be wondering how you can even tell if somebody is influential or not. More and more, standard Twitter applications such as HootSuite (more on this later) display an influence score right in the user profile.

Here are a few tips to get noticed by influential connections:

- If you see an influencer online, say hello to them through a tweet or send them a compliment.
- Re-tweet their content, especially if it is something of vital interest to them such as their business, blog, or favorite charity.
- If they have a blog, comment on it. Bloggers love comments in their community and will usually pay attention to anyone who takes the time to contribute. This will make them much more likely to recognize and respond to you in the Twitter stream.
- Pay attention to their tweets and show helpfulness. For example, if an important potential business contact or thought leader mentions they are going to be in Boston, and you know of a favorite restaurant in Boston, let them know. Now that's a tweet that will get their attention!
- Another technique is to find commonality. Look through their LinkedIn profile for a common

hometown, friend, place of employment, or college. Then find a way to mention this coincidence in a tweet.

- Ask them a direct question. While people may be busy, in general the most influential people on Twitter got there by following the Tao of Twitter, too. They can't resist an opportunity to be authentically helpful. So if you ask a question or ask for help, you're more than likely to get a response, unless it's from a Hollywood type.

Finally I want to emphasize the *authentic* part of authentic helpfulness. The social web tends to amplify personal characteristics. If you're just trying to use people to make a sale or game a Klout score, it's going to come across and define your reputation and personal brand. If you're generous and gracious without expecting anything in return, people will go out of their way to look out for you.

Trust the Tao and be patient. It *will* happen.

CHAPTER FOURTEEN

Advanced Twitter Concepts

Believe it or not, your Twitter journey is just beginning. This chapter contains some more advanced ideas to help you get even more benefits from the platform. If you're a beginner, it might be a good idea to take a month, or even two, to master the basic concepts of the Tao before jumping into these ideas. But if you have a handle on it, here are some new things to try out.

Activity Stream

If you click the "Discover" button at the top of the navigation bar, you'll see a prompt for "Activity." This is a timeline of *all* the Twitter-related activities for *all* your followers. This is mildly interesting and can be a great source for finding new lists and followers to explore, but it is probably not something that needs to be attended to very often.

Advertising Programs

Twitter is making money through three types of promoted content across the site:

- Promoted tweets appear in users' timelines in much the same way that sponsored results are displayed on Google.
- Promoted accounts are displayed to users in the "Who to follow" section of the site, which uses algorithms to suggest accounts popular among users who follow similar accounts.
- Promoted trends offers advertisers the opportunity to take advantage of Twitter's "trending topics" feature, appearing at the top of the list, albeit with a disclaimer. This allows businesses and brands to advertise campaigns, slogans, competitions and more.

Audience Maintenance

When your tribe grows beyond a few hundred people, you will probably want to clean out some of the folks who are not following you back, or those who have become inactive. There are lots of free applications to do this, but it's a rapidly changing scene. My recommendation is to do a Google search, or even a Twitter search, for "Twitter maintenance applications" and find suggestions on the best available applications. There are both paid and free options. It's a good idea to do a little account maintenance once a month.

Brand Pages

Brand pages offer several new features for businesses, most prominently promoted tweets and an enhanced design. A brand can "pin" a promoted tweet to the top of its timeline, making it the first thing a visitor is likely to see. Companies can use this space to promote videos, images, links, and more, within their own page.

Custom Backgrounds

As you explore Twitter, you'll notice that many people have customized their Twitter home pages to include interesting backgrounds and relevant business information. These range from free pages to low-cost websites that allow someone to customize his or her site. It's a good idea to provide business information this way by doing a Google search for "Twitter backgrounds" and finding a service that fits your need and budget. Keep these guidelines in mind:

- This will communicate about your brand, so make sure it reflects well on your business.
- Don't make it look too much like an advertisement.
- Include other ways to connect with you, such as LinkedIn or Facebook.
- At this time, Twitter pages do not link to websites.
- Consider having a local graphic designer do a custom page for you. Find some pages that you like as examples so she has something to go by. You can usually have a custom site done for you for under $200.

If you just want to use a picture of the kids as your background, well, you can do that for free. Go to Settings, find "design" on the left-hand screen, and then upload your favorite photo.

Geolocation or Geotagging

The use of location data in tweets adds a pin to your post to tell people where you are in real time. This is an option in your settings and can be used by certain applications to identify Twitter followers near you. Most people are not using this option.

Legal Implications

Publishing on Twitter creates a permanent and searchable record of your statements. While it's important to be real, it's also important to be careful. My favorite local pizza proprietor was sued for $2 million after posting an unflattering tweet about his advertising agency. Tweets are tiny, but carry the same legal weight as a blog post.

In a corporate environment, lawyers should be involved in determining the social media policy to account for laws and regulations specific to your industry.

I'm not suggesting that you become paranoid, but just be aware that you're always publishing.

Listening Platforms

Once you get above about 300 followers or so, it becomes increasingly difficult to follow the conversations. You'll be facing a daily wall of noise. At this point you need to bring in help by downloading a free or low-cost "listening" platform to organize your conversations.

Some of the leading names in this space include Seesmic, TweetDeck, and HootSuite. I've already mentioned these tools as a way to schedule tweets, save searches, and cut corners on time.

But the primary advantage of these applications is organizing followers into logical groups on Twitter Lists. For example, you might have one called "industry experts" and another called "local friends." That way you can isolate and segment the people you *really* want to listen to and follow their conversations. These apps also have the ability to save searches, so you can see a stream of targeted information of interest to you. There are many other little tricks and useful tools built into these apps to make it much easier and more fun to follow along on Twitter. All have versions for smartphones and the iPad.

Mobile

All major smartphone platforms have free Twitter apps available. This way you can carry Twitter with you wherever you go—and you'll want to. They all provide the opportunity to snap a photo from your phone and attach it to a tweet. This can be a lot of fun to share with your friends! There are many platforms available in smartphone app stores, or download a mobile version of your desktop listening platform.

Search

I covered the idea of search in several sections, and it is certainly extremely easy to use. But to really unlock the power of content on Twitter, it's useful to know some *advanced search operators*. You can easily improve your search results by typing these directions directly into the search box.

Typing this:	Shows you tweets that:
lang:en	Are only in the language "English"
funny movies	Contain both "funny" and "movies." This is the default operator.
"Social Slam"	Contain the exact phrase "Social Slam"
man OR woman	Contain either "man" or "woman" (or both).
Steelers -football	Contain "Steelers" but not "football"
#soslam	Contain the hashtag "#soslam"
from:markwschaefer	Were sent from person "markwschaefer"
to:markwschaefer	Were sent to person "markwschaefer"
@markwschaefer	Reference person "markwschaefer"
"chinese restaurant" near:"chicago"	Contain the exact phrase "Chinese restaurant" and sent near "Chicago"
near:NYC within:15mi	Were sent within 15 miles of "NYC"
"social slam" since:2011-07-30	Contain phrase "social slam" and sent since date "2011-07-30" (year-month-day)
"social slam" -attend ☺	Contain phrase "social slam" but not "attend" with a positive sentiment
flight ☹	Contain the word "flight" with a negative sentiment
Flight ?	Contain the word "flight" and ask a question.
hilarious filter:links	Contain the word "hilarious" and link to a URL

More Search Tips

1. Keep your search as simple as possible. More complex searches miss more tweets.

2. There is often more than one variation of popular hashtags (for example, #FollowFriday and #ff mean the same thing).

3. Sometimes a search won't show you older tweets, because there are too many results. Consider doing one or more searches using the before: and since: date operators.

Social Media Policies

Earlier I suggested that companies can deploy the use of Twitter throughout an organization as a possible competitive advantage. But what constitutes abuse? How much time should employees spend on social media at work? What if employees access inappropriate sites?

All of these questions and many more should be addressed in a social media policy. Every organization should have a policy. Even if employees can't access the social web via company computers, it's likely they are getting online through their smartphones. In one news story, a teacher was disciplined for a comment she made about a student on a site unrelated to her, the student, or the school. So to be fair to everybody, make sure employees know what's expected, and what's at risk.

Here's a website with hundreds of examples of organizational social media policies: http://socialmedia governance.com/policies.php.

Spam

By mid-2009 Twitter was becoming so overrun by hackers and spammers that the service was teetering on being unusable. The company has done a good job cleaning up its act, but the spammers are always coming up with new tricks.

"Spamming" can describe a variety of different behaviors. Here are some common tactics that spam accounts often use:

- Posting harmful links (including links to phishing or malware sites)
- Abusing the @reply or @mention function to post unwanted messages to users
- Creating multiple accounts (either manually or using automated tools)
- Spamming trending topics to try to grab attention
- Repeatedly posting duplicate updates
- Posting links with unrelated tweets
- Aggressive following behavior (for instance, mass following and un-following in order to gain attention)

It would be difficult to provide complete guidelines because the tactics change so often. The problems are usually more in the category of the annoying rather than the dangerous, but you should still actively report undesirable behavior or spam. This action doesn't immediately or definitely cause an account to be suspended, but it's an important tool Twitter uses to identify and investigate spam accounts.

Twitter Blog

Twitter is constantly changing and improving. To keep up with the latest ideas, I recommend following the Official Twitter blog at http://blog.twitter.com/

Verified Accounts

On certain accounts (especially those of celebrities) you'll see a little blue check mark next to the user name. This means that account is the real person. It's so easy to set up fake accounts that this has become necessary for some people who are in the public spotlight.

CHAPTER FIFTEEN

Becoming a Top Cat on Twitter Chats

There is one advanced concept that has exploded in popularity and deserves a special section of its own: Twitter chats.

The idea is very simple. A group of people with a common interest gather together on Twitter at a designated time to share ideas and discussion. The discussion is united by a "hashtag," so that all can follow along. For example, #CMChat gathers people who are in the country music business and #CookingChat brings together cooking enthusiasts. There are chats for every imaginable interest, and the list is growing all the time.

There are several powerful benefits of chats:

- Chats are great places to learn and exchange ideas with like-minded individuals from around the world.

- They are excellent places to meet interesting new contacts. When you find a chat that you like, it would be a good idea to follow these individuals and perhaps even create a list of your favorite chat members.
- Chats can help you gain awareness for your own brand and ideas.
- Participating in chats creates connections and content that can enhance your personal influence.
- A company, brand, or individual can establish a voice of authority by creating and leading a chat.
- Chats have become so popular, some companies are paying advertising fees to sponsor them. Yes, you can make money from a Twitter chat!

So how do you get started?

The first thing to do is find a relevant chat. The best way to keep up with this dynamic list is to do a search for "Twitter chat schedule," and you will find a detailed list of chats by subject, day, and time. It will also list the leaders of the chats and sometimes provide links to the most recent sessions.

Once you pick your chats, there are a couple ways to participate. First, follow the people who run these chats and get their updates on upcoming sessions. When the chat is scheduled to occur, you can search for the designated hashtag in Twitter. The best way to follow along is to use a free service like TweetChat or Twitterfall, platforms specifically designed to enhance your Twitter chat experience. If you're a newcomer, tell people that. They'll usually look after you!

A word of warning: On the most popular chats, the tweets may be coming at a furious rate! It can be challenging to follow along when there are concurrent conversations occurring.

Participation is key for reaping the benefits of Twitter chats. Ask and answer questions, add insight, discuss. These are usually very open and friendly forums, so don't be worried about posting a "stupid" comment or question.

Many times, there are predetermined questions, and the moderator will pose these in the form of this example: Q1 What is the best way to get value from a Twitter chat? Participants answer accordingly: A1 One idea is to participate actively and help newcomers.

Creating Your Own Chat

Hosting your own chat can be a fun and rewarding way to create community around your ideas and subject matter. Let's walk through the steps of creating a new Twitter Chat.

Set Up

First, you should secure a descriptive hashtag. At www.Twubs .com, you can see if your hashtag has already been taken and reserve one for your chat. Once you have a unique name, it would be a good to reserve a Twitter handle for the chat, too.

To promote the chat, you may want to create a home base for your community on Facebook, a LinkedIn group, or a blog, where you can make announcements and post completed conversations.

You'll also need to pick a time and regular date for the chat. Every Monday? The second Tuesday of the month? Find a date that fits your schedule, because, as the moderator, you are creating a long-lasting commitment to your community. Some chat communities have co-moderators, or even shared responsibility among all the members.

Be consistent with your schedule. Biweekly and monthly chats are very difficult to maintain. If your audience wonders if the chat will happen each week, it quickly falls off the radar. If you are serious about the effort, make it a weekly chat.

Planning the Content

In preparation for your first chat, you'll want to personally invite a few friends to get the momentum going. Create enough topic questions ahead of time to propel at least 30 minutes of chat. Involve your community in choosing topics and questions. Other chats may be just free-flowing, with no assigned agenda, just places to meet and touch base.

Many chats feature special guests who help answer questions and engage with participants. So, for example, I have been a guest "speaker" on book chats, marketing chats, and leadership chats, to name a few. If you are asked to be a guest on a chat, be sure to have the prepared questions ahead of time, so you can get ready with at least a few tweetable responses. It can be difficult to keep up with the furious pace of conversation through coherent 140-character responses!

Announce your topic and any guests at least a full day in advance, ideally longer. Your topic or guests are what will cement the event on people's calendars.

Post-Chat and Promotion

As the moderator, you are creating some very valuable, shareable content, so be sure to capture this. There are several free platforms to do this, including RowFeeder, Chirpstory, and Storify. You can post this content on your Facebook page or blog and then promote this content to attract new members.

Promoting a link to your home base in industry publications, social media outlets, and related forums is another way to find people who might be interested in the topic.

Another best practice is to e-mail a transcript to your community members after the chat. This will serve as a reminder of the next chat and also keep people in the loop, even if they miss the event.

During the chat, everyone participating will be tweeting with the hashtag in the tweet. Just the act of having the chat is a great way to promote the event. I'll often pop into a chat when I see an interesting hashtag pop up from a friend. As long as you stick to a consistent schedule and provide interesting content, attendance will pick up over time.

Just like everything else, Twitter chats have limitations. The 140-character maximum can limit the depth of a commentary, and even good ideas can get lost in a big chat. And the sheer volume of tweets does not create an environment for accurate sharing of information. Still, the serendipitous connections you make in these forums are often more important than the actual content of the chat.

CHAPTER SIXTEEN

Is Twitter for Everybody?

This is the big question that eventually gets asked by every person and every company trying Twitter for the first time. In the height of your initial frustrations, you may be wondering . . . is Twitter really for everybody?

Most consultants will tell you, "yes." Indeed, there is probably some legitimate business use or benefit available for everyone and every organization.

But after working with hundreds of business professionals across many diverse businesses, I've come to realize the real answer is no—it's not for everyone.

Here's an example. One of my customers is a brilliant management consultant. An engineer by training, he does not come by marketing instinct naturally, and he asked me to help him.

This is a customer who would be perfect for Twitter:

- Small business owner
- Enormous, global market potential (needs a lot of awareness)
- Small marketing budget
- Selling differentiated personal services
- No time to blog or develop extensive content
- Tech-savvy
- A charming, bright person, with an engaging personality

And yet he *will not tweet*. I coaxed, cajoled, and threatened him. I've trained him patiently and even prescribed a daily Twitter regimen. I demonstrated the power of the platform when I found him a potential new customer on the *very first day* of our operation. He didn't follow up and seems to be quite content with his tweet-free existence.

This may seem strange, but it isn't uncommon. I've found similar resistance from many people who could obviously benefit from this business tool. I asked my client "why," and here is his answer:

I'm not sure why, really. I guess the idle chatter (which is mostly what I seem to see when I log on) just doesn't make any sense to me. There's obviously some self-imposed barrier that I can't or just don't want to cross. You were kind enough to introduce me to Twitter, and I appreciated that. There's the old expression about leading a horse to water. Guess I'm just not that thirsty for Twitter water . . . at least yet.

This type of reaction is not unusual. In fact, I was a Twitter-quitter myself and had to really push through a few weeks of this non-intuitive communication platform before I started to understand it.

What is the difference between a Twitter-lover and Twitter-quitter? Does success on Twitter lend itself to a certain personality type? Some say it favors outgoing people, yet introverts are quick to say that they love the platform as way to connect on their own terms and build quality relationships their own way. Maybe it has something to do with patience. Perhaps the problem is being creeped out by the crowds or by having strangers "follow you."

Honestly, I haven't figured it out, but I do acknowledge the fact that some very intelligent and talented people just don't like Twitter, even when they can see the benefits. So be it.

What About Organizations?

Is there a business case for Twitter for every organization and company? Like nearly every business question, the answer is, "It depends!"

Medical professionals, lawyers, financial managers, and defense contractors may have regulatory limitations on the information they can discuss in public. Remember, Twitter is a form of publishing.

And yet, I believe most companies can find their Twitter Happy Place, even in a regulated business. I met my friend Jeff Reed through a LinkedIn group. Jeff works as a wealth adviser for a large national company, but has been hamstrung in his attempts to use social media.

"I am forbidden to use it," he told me. "The company is trying to figure out what to do, but in the meantime I feel like the world is passing me by."

Regulated industries, like banking and healthcare, have to pay attention to the legal ramifications of how they share information. The law is the law. Still, I think they are missing a bigger opportunity by not exploring how social media can be used on a very personal and human level.

I asked Jeff, "Does your company forbid you from attending a business networking meeting?"

"No."

"Do they keep you away from going to a chamber of commerce function?"

"No."

"When you go to these meetings, do they tell you what you can and can't say?"

"No."

"Then what's the difference? This is just another business networking opportunity. You don't have to sell, you don't have to advise. You don't even have to identify your employer. Why not just be yourself and meet cool people and learn from them? Who knows . . . they just might turn into clients some day."

This got Jeff's attention. He was interested enough to enroll in one of my college classes, and from that point on he has been on fire with social networking, exploring several strategies to connect with people in meaningful new ways. And it's working! He has even been named as an internal social media advisor to his own company. They are creating competitive advantage through social media in a regulated industry.

If you are expected to grow your business through time-consuming live networking meetings or expensive advertising programs, doesn't it make sense to unleash the powerful, cost-effective potential of the social web . . . before your competitors do?

When it comes to business communications strategy, it really gets down to this: What are your business objectives? What do you need to say? Where do your customers get their information?

If your customers are not engaging in this platform you're going to waste a big wad of time on Twitter and get frustrated.

But I want to suggest two big *howevers* before you decide your business is not cut out for Twitter.

However, you may not really know where your customers are getting their information, even if you think you do! People are piling on to the social web in record numbers and are also spending an enormous amount of time there. In an always-connected world, the role of social media in the business and personal world is blurring.

I had a client who resisted Twitter because she insisted that her customers had no interest in it. I conducted some customer research for her—completely unrelated to Twitter—and discovered that "social media" was the number one marketing and business issue for the majority of her customers! By getting in front of the curve and mastering Twitter before her customers were immersed in it, she was able to guide them, position herself as a subject-matter expert, and even create some new business opportunities for her company.

Now for *however* number two. *However,* there are *many* other business benefits to Twitter beyond simply getting sales leads. Even if your customers aren't there in force, it is still an incredibly powerful way to listen, learn, connect with thought leaders, and identify new business opportunities.

I have seen an array of diverse organizations thrive on Twitter, from Realtors to florists, from mega-brands to my handyman (whom I found on Twitter). Colleges, hospitals, non-profits, health professionals, shipping companies, government agencies, and utilities have all realized business gains from a Twitter presence.

There's a reason I placed this chapter near the end of the book. By now you have learned about the transformational power of this platform and have read some inspiring success stories. It's not so easy to quit now, is it? There are just so many ways to define success, create wealth, discover benefits, and even have fun with Twitter.

OK, let's bring it home. It's time to put it all together.

CHAPTER SEVENTEEN

Tao Power: Putting It All Together

One night I was observing a Twitter conversation going back and forth between a woman named Amy Howell (@howellmarketing) and several marketing professionals in my tribe.

Amy seemed enthusiastic (uses lots of !!!), supportive, intelligent, and fun. From her professional and complete Twitter profile, I could tell she runs a public relations and marketing firm in my home state of Tennessee. The link to her website also showed me that we share many interests and that she is a fellow blogger. Perhaps there were opportunities for business synergy?

Amy and I had connected—we were following each other on Twitter—but we had not really *connected*. She seemed like a person I would like to get to know and possibly even do business with, so I made a conscious decision to get to know her and hopefully add her to my tribe. Over the next few weeks I . . .

- Looked for opportunities just to say hello and compliment her when I saw her online.
- Read her tweets and, when I saw interesting content, re-tweeted it to my followers.
- Started reading her blog, commented on it, and, in an act of authentic helpfulness, tweeted a link to her blog to the people who follow me. This helped promote her efforts.

Soon, Amy and I were having regular conversations over Twitter. We grew to like each other, and she appreciated the support I gave her by tweeting her links and blog posts. She started to return the favor and quickly became an online friend and loyal reader of my blog.

As I often do, I invited my new Twitter friend to talk on the phone. In this age of conversation-avoidance, a phone call seems like a luxury, but I think it is an essential part of building and cementing strong new business relationships, especially if a live meeting is improbable.

In our call, Amy mentioned that she had an upcoming meeting in my hometown of Knoxville and that she to stay overnight to have dinner with me and my wife. I couldn't have been more pleased and excited to finally meet my new friend.

But a conflict arose. I had committed to a speaking engagement at a regional marketing meeting and the time of the event had been moved to the exact day Amy was to be in town. I had an idea—wouldn't Amy make a great addition to the panel discussion? Everyone agreed, and Amy became an important part of the program, giving her the chance to network with a host of relevant business professionals. She was extremely grateful for this important professional exposure and my authentic helpfulness.

After the event, we had dinner, and Amy mentioned she was part of a group of fellow marketers and bloggers called the Social CMO. The group was going to attend a conference she was planning in Memphis and then meet to discuss ways to work together. It sounded like fun, and shortly, through Amy's recommendation, I became part of the group.

On my way to Amy's Memphis meeting, I had to drive through Nashville during the traditional lunch hour and decided to reach out to a new Twitter friend named Laura Click (@lauraclick), who lived in that city. Although I did not know her very well, I invited her to meet for lunch, since I was nearby. Laura and I hit it off, and the meeting started an important business relationship for me—Laura has since helped me with client writing assignments, contributed a guest blog post, helped me write a chapter for a book, and collaborated on a charity effort. She has

become one of my most important business partners.
As my business grew, I actually moved several of my
customers over to her when she started her own consulting
business, helping her jump-start her career.

When I arrived in Memphis for the Social CMO, it was
great fun meeting many Twitter friends for the first time.
One of them was Glen Gilmore (@glengilmore), a well-
known New Jersey attorney and one of Amy's strategic
partners. Months later I was in a position to recommend
my new friend Glen for a teaching position at his alma
mater, Rutgers University—a thrill for both of us.

I also got to meet dozens of other thought leaders
like Jeremy Victor (@jeremyvictor), Billy Mitchell
(@billymitchell1), and Ryan Sauers (@ryansauers), who
have become close friends and business collaborators.

Amy and I continue to find business opportunities for
each other and partner in many ways . . . and we always
will. None of this would have happened without the Tao
Power of connections, content, and helpfulness. This is
how it works.

The Tao Movement

Since the first edition of this book came out in 2011, *The
Tao of Twitter* has inspired countless readers and sparked
thousands of new business benefits. It is not just a book. It
is becoming a movement.

An example of this came through an e-mail I received from Welsh businessman Tony Dowling. I had never heard of Tony before, but the subject line of his message got my attention: "How One Book Changed My Life." Here's what he had to say:

Dear Mark,

There I was, minding my own business. Raising my family, working hard, and generally trying to enjoy life, when along came an amazing book, a book that has changed my life. Not in some scarily enormous unbelievable way, but in small and elegant and permanent ways. I read *The Tao of Twitter,* and things started to happen. Things that were good.

I'm 42 years old and consider myself the luckiest guy in the world. I run a commercial radio station in the U.K., a pretty big and successful one. I have an amazing wife, we have been together for 20-odd years and still feel like we did when we first met. I also have two amazing children and, largely because of those two little guys, I thought life couldn't be better.

Turns out I was wrong.

I read *The Tao of Twitter* around three months ago and was immediately inspired. As a media owner, I like to keep up with the changes in the world of marketing, advertising, and communications, so I devour books like *Tao* regularly, but never has one struck me so deeply and so quickly.

I had a flash of inspiration—a genuine, physical feeling—that hit me around the part of the book that talks about "authentic helpfulness." I decided that I was going to try to follow this path, to stop selling and be selfless . . . to give back to the universe.

I was going to start out in social media, build a blog, and use *Tao* as my guide.

I decided to blog about what I know and freely give away all the knowledge I had. My blog is literally called "Completely Free Sales Advice." I put my heart into it and created a lot of content quickly—a collection of my thoughts about selling, advertising, and marketing. Readers started to appear, as if by magic.

Using techniques lifted directly from the book, I slowly built an audience for the blog through Twitter, and that audience started to become a community, becoming more involved in the discussions.

At first, many of my existing contacts came forward and asked for help. Then, they started to encourage others to join in. After only a few dozen blogs, I had around 15 "clients" forming a community around "Completely Free Sales Advice."

What has amazed me the most is the almost perfect predictions the book makes about the journey I have undertaken.

Over the months, word continued to spread, through Twitter of course, and Facebook, too. And now readers are connecting through my words and are beginning to help each other! Everyone is taking part. The authentic helpfulness is spreading, and so are the business benefits.

The people following the blog are slowly but surely melding into a genuine community— interested only in helping each other out. Some of these people have become my good friends, people who have challenged me and inspired me through their own authentic helpfulness.

And together, we are beginning to collaborate and create new business benefits. Pippa Davies (a blogger, psychologist, and creativity expert) and I have formed an informal alliance to help each other improve our writing, share best practices, and realize more traffic to both of our sites. My new social media friend has, in turn, introduced me to numerous contacts that have become invaluable business partners in my "proper job" at the radio station. And more amazing, she has put me in contact with professionals who will help me care for my beautiful autistic little boy.

Dr. Sarah Bruton, an entrepreneur running a local spa business, is beginning to keep a record of the measurable, positive differences we have made in revenue, genuine ROI, and other tangible benefits from the social-media lessons we have learned from *The Tao of Twitter.* Sarah will be my first guest poster, as she details the benefits she has gained from taking part.

The list goes on and on. All of this goodness seemed to come out of the blue. Learning the lessons of *The Tao of Twitter* has immediately paid me back for whatever small help I have managed to provide to anyone else.

So thank you Mark. Thank you because *The Tao of Twitter* is changing my life every day in small ways and is giving me the inspiration to change it in big ways, too.

With appreciation,

Tony Dowling

I was moved by this letter, and so naturally began to connect with Tony on Twitter. Day by day, he reported on his increasing Tao-related successes, and I finally suggested (through a tweet) that he should create a social media conference in Wales to gather this wonderful community together. "We'll do it!" he said.

Within 24 hours he had 10 volunteers, an outline for an agenda, and his first sponsor. Within three days he had a venue (the amazing Celtic Manor Resort), funding from the Welsh government, and his first guest speaker—me. There was no way I was going to miss the world's first Tao of Twitter Conference. Who knows how far it will go or where it will lead?

By now, I hope you can see this undeniable pattern of connections, content, and authentic helpfulness running through every success story. And while it has created surprising and amazing benefits, in the long term the most important payoff will be the relationships I've formed with the many wonderful people I've mentioned, like Michelle Chmielewski, Aaron Killian, Amy Howell, and Tony Dowling, plus the hundreds of other people who have followed the Tao of Twitter. It can happen for you, too.

I want to end this book the same way I end all of my social media marketing classes—with a quote from a university student who left this comment on my blog:

> Social media marketing is not something that
> can be taught—it has to be experienced, and
> this is why schools have a hard time teaching

classes about it. Students who take advantage
of social media will have a leg up on those who
do not. Formal education and books can show
you the tools . . . but it is up to YOU to learn
how to apply them for you and your business.

I'm so grateful that you've read my book. But no
matter how many times you return to it, you can't master
the Tao of Twitter until you immerse yourself in it and
learn by doing. So I want to encourage you to be persistent,
patient, and present.

Best of luck as you find your own path, your own Tao,
on your lifetime Twitter adventure.

Acknowledgments

The story of any Twitter journey is one of friendships.
I have dozens of wonderful tales about hundreds of
people I could have included in this book. My love and
deepest respect goes out to my Twitter Tribe, students, and
customers. You have changed my life in amazing ways.

To my offline family, Ryan, Lauren, Avery, and
Hannah. Thank you for your support and patience while I
was buried in my laptop. Their role in my life had nothing
to do with Twitter.

My dear love Rebecca, the queen of my life—Thank
you!

Most important, I thank God for His patience with
this broken servant, and for granting me the opportunity to
glorify Him through this work.

About the Author

Mark W. Schaefer is a globally recognized educator, business consultant, and author, who blogs at {grow}—one of the top marketing blogs in the world. Mark has worked in global sales, PR, and marketing positions for nearly 30 years and now provides consulting services as Executive Director of U.S.-based Schaefer Marketing Solutions. His clients include companies of all sizes, from start-ups to global brands.

Mark has advanced degrees in marketing and organizational development and holds seven patents. He is a faculty member of the graduate studies program at Rutgers University and is the founder of Social Slam, a national social media event that takes place each April. He is the author of the best-selling book *Return On Influence*. He has received numerous industry awards and was named by *Forbes* magazine as one of the Top 50 social media "power influencers" of the world.

Follow Mark on the web:

Blog: www.businessesGROW.com
Twitter: @markwschaefer
Facebook: http://on.fb.me/markwschaefer
LinkedIn: http://linkd.in/mwschaefer
YouTube: http://bit.ly/yt-schaefer

Notes

Chapter Four

1. http://blog.cmbinfo.com/press-center-content/bid/46920/
Consumers-Engaged-Via-Social-Media-Are-More-Likely-To
-Buy-Recommend

2. http://www.mediapost.com/publications/?fa = Articles
.showArticle&art_aid = 133837&nid = 117809

3. http://www.businessinsider.com/twitter-destroys-facebook
-2010-12

4. http://www.emarketer.com/Article.aspx?R = 1007639

5. http://images.businessweek.com/ss/08/09/0908_micro
blogceo/index.htm

6. http://www.exacttarget.com/

7. http://brandsavant.com/why-twitter-is-bigger-than-you
-think/

Chapter Five

1. http://firstmonday.org/htbin/cgiwrap/bin/ojs/index.php/
fm/article/view/2317/2063

Chapter Six

1. If you're completely new to Twitter and unfamiliar with terms such as "direct message" or "Follow Friday" don't worry! These are explained in the strategy section under the Language of Twitter in Chapter 8.

Chapter Eight

1. http://www.businessesgrow.com/2009/07/13/twitter-for -business-four-breakthrough-insights/

Chapter Nine

1. Some of these ideas came from my friend, entrepreneur and blogger Neicole Crepeau: http://nmc.itdevworks.com/ index.php/2009/10/5-cleveruses-for-lists/

Index